The
Songwriter's
Handbook

The Songwriter's Handbook

**by
Harvey
Rachlin**

FUNK & WAGNALLS   NEW YORK

Designed by Joy Chu

Manufactured in the United States of America

Library of Congress Cataloging in Publication Data

Rachlin, Harvey.
The songwriter's handbook.

Includes index.
1. Music, Popular (Songs, etc)–Writing and
publishing I. Title.
MT67.R2   784'.028   77-2946
ISBN 0-308-10321-1

89 90 20 19 18 17 16 15 14 13 12

**To the gang——
Phil, Mazie, Steven,
Craig, and Gary**

I am particularly indebted to two people in the preparation of this book: Gary F. Roth and Bernard Skydell. The assistance of both these gentlemen was most invaluable.

I would also like to express my special gratitude to Albert Berman, Syde Berman, Alfred Haber, Walter Hofer, Irwin Robinson, and Paula Schack. Finally, I am grateful to the following organizations for their kind contributions: American Society of Composers, Authors and Publishers; Broadcast Music, Inc.; SESAC Inc.; and the American Guild of Authors and Composers. The particular individuals from these organizations are Nicholas Arcomano, Lewis Bachman, Albert F. Ciancimino, Ervin Drake, Bruce Gold, I. Fred Koenigsberg, and Walter Wager.

Contents

righting Musical Compositions / The Copyright Notice / Copyright Registration of Unpublished Song Collections / Copyright Infringement of Musical Compositions / Copyrighting Sound Recordings / Notice of Use of Copyrighted Music on Mechanical Instruments

Foreword
by Sammy Cahn

WHEN MOST PEOPLE listen to songs, they seldom care who wrote them. *I do!* The fact is *I Should Care!* (Check copyright owner!) The chances are that I may well have written one of them.

It has been said that everyone in the world has an occupation and a preoccupation—songwriting. At one point or another we all feel the urge to express ourselves with song, a lyric perhaps to enunciate elation at falling in love, or a melancholy melody to indicate insecurity at falling out of love.

For me, personally, there is no more satisfying or greater profession than the successful songwriter. Whenever I lecture in a college I tell the students that the rewards are endless (check ASCAP royalties!). One time a student, during a Q & A period, said, "Mr. Cahn, what is wrong with pursuing a successful architectural career?" I said, "Nothing! But who walks down the street humming a building?"

Songs are magical things and I sincerely believe there is no way for a good song to remain unknown. For instance, I wrote "If It's the Last Thing I Do" forty years ago with Saul Chaplin and it just hit all the charts, thanks to Thelma Houston. Can you imagine the great satisfaction it must be to write something that may remain forever, bringing pleasure to someone yet unborn?

As long as there are people there will be songs because songs like people never change! There may be new sounds and new ways, but underneath it all there will always be the need for the happy song (check ''Singin' in the Rain'') and the need for the song of unrequited love (check Sinatra!). Any song is an extension of the human emotion whatever that emotion may be.

Like any profession success in songwriting requires total dedication, and with dedication comes skill. Which at long last brings me to the reason for this foreword. I sincerely believe this book will be highly useful and most informative not only to the amateur but to the professional creator as well. Read it! Study it! Learn it! It may well get you to where you are going, and much, much faster!

''As Long as There's Music'' there will be songwriters. If you are a songwriter with ''High Hopes'' (is there any other kind?) this book is vital to you. It's no ''Pocketful of Miracles,'' but as far as teaching the rudiments and the facets of today's music business it has ''The Best of Everything'' and may well help you go ''All the Way!'' It has ''Style'' and was written with a ''Touch of Class.'' When you write songs, you may find it impossible and difficult and frustrating, and you will, now and again, feel like giving up. *Don't!* (Check ''High Hopes!'') This book will add information to your dedication and information and dedication are like the horse and carriage in ''Love & Marriage,'' and like the lyricist said, ''Ya can't have one without the other!''

Beverly Hills, California
4 June 1977

Author's Note: Sammy Cahn is one of the great songwriters of all time. I consider him ''the lyricists' lyricist!'' Mr. Cahn has won four Academy Awards for his ''Call Me Irresponsible,'' ''High Hopes,'' ''All the Way,'' and ''3 Coins in the Fountain.'' He won the only Emmy ever given to a song (''Love & Marriage''). He is the president of the Songwriters' Hall of Fame, a member of the board of directors at ASCAP, and totally dedicated to all things words & music!

Introduction

THE SONGWRITER'S HANDBOOK has been written for all song-writers—professionals and amateurs alike—who want a better understanding of their craft and of the music business.

This book will prove to be of great value to those songwriters who have written a song and are unsure of what the next steps are: how to copyright their song, how to prepare it for an audition, who to audition it for, and where to reach these important individuals who should comprise the songwriter's "Top 40" people to contact.

Other songwriters, more experienced in practice, will find the book equally beneficial. These are songwriters who have been writing for years and have been unsuccessful in their attempts to get their songs recorded. These individuals need assistance—whether it be in reworking their material or in obtaining a better understanding of music business procedures.

Finally, professional songwriters will find the material contained herein very useful. Information on the new copyright law, writing music for the different types of media, and starting music publishing and recording companies will prove to be an important supplement to the knowledge and experience they have built up over the years.

Here then is a comprehensive book on songwriting which covers the entire spectrum of the profession, from the conception of lyric ideas and melodies to the operation of the forces that ultimately guide and control the songwriter's creations.

The Songwriter's Handbook is about writing and marketing

songs in today's competitive music business. It is hoped that the reader will realize the book's underlying theme: exposure through education. If you are trying to get your songs commercially recorded then you obviously feel they are of high quality. Now you must learn how to give them the proper exposure.

The content is in simple, down-to-earth terms, and will prepare you, the songwriter, to walk on the road just as it is. It is up to you to make a concerted effort to read, study, and put into use the information that lies ahead.

Start walking.

—Harvey Rachlin

"Press on: Nothing in the world can take the place of persistence. Talent will not; nothing is more common than unsuccessful men with talent. Genius will not; unrewarded genius is almost a proverb. Education will not; the world is full of educated derelicts. Persistence and determination alone are omnipotent."

The
Songwriter's
Handbook

1: Words and Music

SONGWRITING IS an artistic process. A large portion of it necessitates talent—and talent cannot be taught. But songwriting is also a craft—and that can be taught. Songs are bound by a beginning, middle, and end; musical notes, which contain both pitch and rhythmic value; and language. These are tangible elements contained within a definitive structure for which rules can be made and taught.

Essentially, the elements of the popular song are:

Language
1. The title
2. The lyric

Music
3. The melody
4. The rhythm
5. The harmony.

These elements can be found in all songs except, of course, instrumentals which contain no lyrics. The conception and construction of these elements are influenced by our personality, experiences, imagination, intelligence, and education.

The study of composition has been a universal and timeless pursuit. Even the greatest composers in history took time out for this endeavor. Mozart and Bach, for instance, are two among the many masters who performed the task that all songwriters of today should:

they analyzed the works of their contemporaries. They even went to such lengths as to write out the scores of these writers so that they might assimilate their techniques. George Gershwin went all the way to Paris to seek permission from the great Ravel to study with him. And Burt Bacharach studied composition with several teachers after writing his first song at the age of twenty-one.

Never think that the study of other composers' songs will damage your creative potential. There is a tremendous reservoir available to learn from every day. The songs you hear on the radio daily should serve as your guide, as they are the most current examples of what a successful song is, their popularity indicated by their rise and fall on the "record charts." Listen to how others have reached the public, for that is your aim, too.

If the public is the frontier—the unexplored, fertile region to be musically tapped—then the charts are the maps, and you, the songwriter, are the pioneer.

Writing Commercial Song Lyrics

The commercial song lyric is all around us. Turn on the radio and you can hear it. Go into a record store and you can buy it. Buy the sheet music and you can see it. Sing the song and you can feel it. So what is it? Let's first examine what "commercial" is and then we will discuss it as it applies to the song lyric.

Commercial is what has mass appeal, what people are buying. The majority of the record-buying public is largely the youth of today's society—those between nine and twenty–four years of age. They help determine what's played on the radio and what's not, which groups will make the next nationwide concert tour and which won't. They are the target of the music industry because they are endowed with the one very potent force the music business could not sustain itself without—purchase power.

You, as a songwriter, should cater to the whims and tastes of the masses. They are the ones who keep the record companies in business, who in turn keep the producers in business, who in turn keep the publishers in business, who in turn keep the songwriters eating.

The commercial song lyric, therefore, is one that is expressed in today's language and that many people will like (probably relate to) and buy. But this is too simple for our understanding. The elements that comprise a successful song lyric must be examined.

The Title

People in the music business will tell you how important an original catchy title is in order to make a hit song. Then you'll read the charts and see a song with a common title like "I Want You" climbing to the top. Common or previously used titles, however, are generally exceptions to what we find at the top of the charts. A songwriter should not use the same title to his song as one that has achieved such a widespread degree of public recognition that it stands out as distinguishing that particular song from all others.

Study the charts and examine the titles. Determine what is eye-catching, catchy-sounding, and unique about those up-and-coming future hits. This will help your understanding of what's commercial.

A song's title is important and you should never underestimate its value. It can add leverage to placing your song with a recording artist and the song's future commercial success. It can be a cliché ([I Never Promised You A] "Rose Garden"); message ("What the World Needs Now Is Love"); something everybody can identify with ("We've Only Just Begun"); catchy ("Tie a Yellow Ribbon Round the Ole Oak Tree"); novel ("The Streak"); provocative ("Me and Mrs. Jones"); or suggestive ("Come a Little Bit Closer"). The title will depend on the lyrical content, of course, and, as we find in today's market, is often repeated throughout the song in the form of a "hook" (see page 12).

The title, like the lyric, should not be offensive, but be something people can easily grab onto—something memorable. Many times an artist will turn down a new song just because the title might conflict with his image. He may not even wish to listen to the songwriter's demo. The title will be the first line of communication your song has with those who audition it. Make it the beginning.

The Lyric

There are certain aspects of the lyric that require examination. The following are some general rules you should keep in mind when writing lyrics:

1 *Devote the lyric to a popular subject* like love or the pursuit

of happiness. Stay away from drugs, war, explicit sex, and other offensive subjects.

2. *Don't make the lyric too personal*. If you are writing about a love affair you had, will the average listener be able to relate to it?

3. *Innovation*. Try to have the lyrics say something new or something old in a new way.

4. *Clarity*. Get your point across. Say it in down-to-earth terms, and don't go off on tangents with several unrelated ideas.

5. *Imagery*. Paint a picture in the listener's mind. Make him *see* as well as *feel* what's going on.

6. *Climax*. Surprise endings, twists, play-on-words always get a favorable response.

7. *Rhyme*. Rhymes don't have to be exact but don't stray too far.

8. *Avoid excess wordage*. Say what you want in as few words as possible.

9. *Appeal*. The lyric should attract the listener's attention.

10. *Strong construction*. Every line of the lyric should be an integral part of the whole.

11. *Movement*. Each section of the lyric should flow into the next.

Now, let's examine the elements of the lyric:

1. *Theme*. Your song should have a solid theme, a premise that is easy to understand. But this is more a common denominator than a rule. The success of some songs is partially determined by their vagueness, their ambiguity, guessing what the author is trying to say.

2. *Beginning and end*. Each of these aspects should be solid. The music can be great, but if the lyric doesn't get into it right away, the song might just as well end there. And the ending should make a statement that leaves a strong feeling remaining with the listener.

3. *Content*. A song's theme can be expressed in a variety of forms. Story and message songs are among two of the most popular forms. Whichever way you choose, be sure to write it lyrically, not poetically. You may, however, want to make use of devices common to other forms of literature in the lyric (and title). The lyrics in the following songs (and as illustrated by their titles) make use of the literary device that precedes the title: metaphor ("I Married an Angel"); simile ("Loves Me Like a Rock"); euphemism ("House of the Ris-

ing Sun''); satire (''Cat's in the Cradle''); and onomatopoeia
(''Splish Splash'').

One of the ways to capture your idea is through phrases that are
repeated throughout the song. This is referred to as the ''hook,'' and
lyrically speaking, it is the time to say whatever it is you wish to get
across.

Whatever it is you say, be sure to say it in today's language.
This is what commercialism is all about. The themes and stories of
songs haven't changed since the very first ones; it's the way they are
said. Listen to the radio and begin (if you haven't already) to think
and write in today's terms.

Setting a Lyric to Music

Many of the greatest songs have been written where the composer played a melody for the lyricist with the hope that a lyric would
be written that would complement the music. It isn't just talent alone
that enables the successful lyricist to come up with the right words
every time. He knows his craft and follows general principles when
he writes.

When setting a lyric to music, be aware of the following points:

1. *Classification*. A song's commercial classification will dictate certain styling and particular ways of saying things. For instance,
a lyricist styling the thoughts of a man making a suggestion to a
woman would tailor the suggestion according to the mode of the
song. For a rhythm and blues song, he might express it by saying
''Let's Get Down,'' whereas in a country and western song he might
use ''I Want to Touch Your Heart.''

Determine the classification your song belongs to and tailor your
lyric to use the language and idioms of that particular category. Most
contemporary songs can be found to belong to one of the following
categories: pop, country and western, rhythm and blues (soul), rock
'n' roll, easy listening (middle of the road), folk, gospel, jazz,
disco, and children's.

2. *Mood (Harmony)*. Have the lyric follow the mood of the
music. Generally, match notes in the melody harmonized by minor

sounding (sad) chords with words that reflect that sentiment and notes in the melody harmonized by major sounding (bright) chords with words that reflect that sentiment. Variations in the harmony underlie the mood of the song.

3. *Structure.* The music for which you will be writing lyrics will have a certain pattern or structure. This will either be in the form of two verses, a bridge, and a verse again (AABA); verse, chorus, verse, chorus (ABAB); or some variation of these. You will pattern your lyric to fit the particular musical structure at hand.

4. *Length.* You have a limited time period to convey the lyric to the listener. Be concise and to the point.

5. *Follow the notes.* Certain notes in a melody are stressed or accented as, for instance, a leap to a high note or a note on a strong beat. Certain words lend themselves to be used in these instances. For example, in the Burt Bacharach-Hal David tune "I Say a Little Prayer," the word "up" is used in the first line against a large leap in the melody. Be sure not to use unimportant words or syllables against strong beats or sustained notes of the melody.

6. *Meter.* Be sure the words fit into the music's rhythmic pulse.

7. *Blend.* The lyric and music must sound as if they fit one another—like a marriage made in heaven. Each must complement the other.

8. *Make the lyric easy to sing.* Certain vowels or syllables do not come out clearly when sung with certain musical phrases or (high) notes. Avoid this.

How to Find and Develop Ideas for Lyrics

One of the best ways to find ideas for lyrics is to stay on top of current events. Your daily life provides a storehouse of potential themes, ideas, and subjects. Each day we are bombarded by newspapers, motion pictures, television, books, magazines, stories, etc. From these, the basis for a lyric can be constructed from headlines, articles of human interest, or conversation from dramas, comedies, or your next-door neighbor.

A cliché or phrase is often the basis for a lyric. You can write a lyric using an old one, capitalizing on a current one, or inventing your own. Perhaps a dramatic episode from a friend's life could be developed into a story lyric, or a lesson you learned could become the basis for a message lyric. Or someone you know, for example, expressed a birthday wish in an original manner that could be the basis for a new birthday song. Of course, your own emotional experiences will often be the source of inspiration for your next lyric, but if you are writing about another love affair, be sure to say it with a new slant. The ability to take that which happens in our daily lives and transform it lyrically into a commercial story or message is the mark of the gifted lyric craftsman.

Many of the most successful lyricists use the same method to develop their ideas, thoughts, and lines into lyrics. They write a short story using and building around these elements. Such a composition would have a discernible beginning, middle, and end with a readily identifiable theme. Specific lines they wish to have in the lyric are used within the story either as conversation or narration. They then rework the composition and add new ideas and lines until it is complete. From this they construct a lyric, paying attention to such elements as structure (pattern), rhyme, and meter. Since the ideas have already been worked out, it is now a matter of stating the story or message lyrically.

In conclusion, the commercial lyric is generally one that is a concise story or message told in today's terms and is "married" to the melody. It creates an emotional response, is memorable, easy to relate to, and has strong construction.

Writing Music

As noted earlier, the music of popular songs is comprised of three elements: melody, rhythm, and harmony. With only twelve different musical notes available to us and a relatively small number of rhythmic patterns basic to most songs, there is surprisingly an almost infinite number of possibilities open to writers on the kind of music they can create. Yet, because we are so greatly influenced by what we hear and what we like, it is no wonder that we tend to write songs that sound like many of today's hitmakers. Listeners also tend to take faster to songs reminiscent of the last record they purchased.

By examining melody, rhythm, and harmony, we will see how the creation, repetition, and variation of these elements combine to form the popular song.

Melody

To discuss what's more important in a song, the lyric or melody, would be futile, since so many people are divided on this and it's a matter of personal taste. For some people it's the "beat" that determines whether or not they like the song. In any case, the melody is extremely important and requires examination.

The melody of a song should be catchy and easy to sing. There are some general rules regarding melody that are common to popular songs which the composer should keep in mind. These are:

1. *Melodic pattern*. A song should have a pattern or form to it. This means the repetition of a limited amount of phrases or musical ideas contrasted by the repetition of others.

2. *Range*. Every person has a limit as to the lowest and highest note he or she can sing. You should always try to write your songs within the range of the average singer.

3. *"Get into it" soon*. If the meat of your melody begins too late, people won't want to wait to hear it. A good commercial song will "get into it" quickly.

4. *Modulation*. Depending on the song's pattern, the composer may wish to modulate (change keys) some of his musical ideas. This serves to enhance the song and prevents the listener from getting bored.

5. *Length*. A commercial song usually runs no longer than three and a half minutes. A longer song will present a problem to the radio station program director who desires short songs and a lot of commercial advertisements.

6. *Climax*. Many songs reach a climax, the most intense part of the melody, usually found near the end of the song, and which can be a high or sustained note.

7. *Harmony*. The chords should musically correspond to and enhance the melody.

8. *Simplicity*. Simplicity is the best rule to follow when composing. Simple melodies are more memorable and easier to sing.

9. *Keep your melody commercial*. That is, your melody should

have today's sound. It is a shame so many amateur composers write "dated" songs. Make your melody interesting and contemporary.

Structure

Successful songs are memorable because they are not complicated. There is a pattern or form to them that makes them easy to remember. Inherent to a song's form are the elements of repetition and contrast.

Repetition is the repeating of a musical section. Likewise, the corresponding chord progression and lyric meter also repeat. After this section is repeated, a different musical section is offered, and is followed either by a return to the original or to another one with the consequent return to the original section.

The most common form of repetition is the AABA pattern. This contains two (A) sections of the same musical idea (verse), a (B) section of a different idea (bridge), and then a return to the original (A) idea. They are usually sections of eight bars each, making up the common thirty-two-bar refrain. Some songs have a (C) section of a third, different musical idea.

There are variations of the AABA pattern and some of the most common ones are: AB, ABAC, and AA. The B section of a song should always complement the A section, just as the lyric should complement the melody. It can be a modulation to major or minor mode, thereby offering a change of melodic mood and/or a change of rhythm (tempo), thereby creating a different "feel."

Although the thirty-two-bar (AABA pattern) song has been the conventional form, you should not feel compelled to use it if it is not suited for your song. Today, more than ever, songs depart from that pattern. Nor are you restricted to keep the same time signature throughout your song. These are general rules and rules are made to be broken. But before you break them you have to know what they are. Burt Bacharach is a master at sneaking a two-quarter measure in a song that starts and continues for some length in four-quarter time.

Range and Key

You should gear your songs to be sung by the average person. Therefore, you will want to have a range written within average limits and a key devised for average singing ability. A good melody will generally have a minimum range of one octave, but shouldn't surpass a perfect twelfth. This means a range of one octave plus a perfect fifth. Musically (in the treble clef), this looks like:

Example 1　　　　　　*Example 2*

In the first example, the note F is a perfect fifth above the octave of low B-flat and in the second, the note G is a perfect fifth above the octave of low C. You should try to keep your songs within these limits; otherwise you might find professional singers will not be able to perform them, no less the general public who will be less capable.

The easiest and most popular keys songs are written in are C (no sharps or flats) and keys of one or two sharps (G and D) or one or two flats (F or B♭). Avoid use of a lot of chromatics (notes alien to the key), extreme leaps in melody, and difficult key signatures.

Rhythm

Rhythm is a musical element inherent to every song. With only a few notes of fixed rhythmic value, there is almost an infinite amount of rhythmic combinations available to the composer, although only a small number of variations are found to be basic to most popular songs.

Rhythm has also been referred to as the beat, tempo, meter, groove, or "sound," and it helps create the song's "feel." The song's "feel" can come from sources other than a drum beat. A moving bass line or the strum of the rhythm guitar, for example, can also establish it.

For many songs, especially dance forms like discotheque music, the beat is essential. In these songs the melody and lyric are often less important than the groove the song creates. They are designed primarily to be danced to and the dancer is concerned more with the rhythm than the words and music. The rhythm of other dance forms, such as the waltz (three-quarter time), fox trot (four-quarter time), or polka (six-eight time) is also essential.

Harmony

Harmony is the combination of musical notes or chords played against the melody and serves to enhance it.

Harmony plays an important role in the songwriter's compositions. The music writer who lacks harmonic knowledge is limited in the scope and beauty his songs can possess. It is like being the lyricist whose lyrical vocabulary is limited. Of course, there are successful songwriters who cannot read or write a note of music, but there are very few of those, and unless you fall into their class, you will need training like the rest of us, including Mozart, Gershwin, and Bacharach.

If you do not have training in this area, you should begin at once. Books on elementary music theory, private instruction, or a music theory or harmony class will train you. And you will see how enlarging your harmonic vocabulary will strengthen your melody writing abilities. Such instruction should include the study of basic chords and their variants: major, minor, dominant sevenths, diminished, augmented, thirteenths, suspended, etc. It will also help you to better play and analyze those songs you select and train you to write your own lead sheets, if you cannot already do so.

Setting Music to a Lyric

In setting music to a lyric already written, you will follow many of the rules set forth in "Setting a Lyric to Music." Your music should originate after careful examination of the lyric:

1. *Classification.* An idea or particular lines from a lyric may require a certain type of music to be set to it.

2. *Mood.* Match certain lyrical phrases with conducive harmonies.

3. *Structure.* Decide what the lyric structure is in terms of verses, bridges, and choruses, and pattern your lyric to fit this.

4. *Length.* You have a limited amount of time to complete the music. Be concise and limit the amount of musical ideas.

5. *Follow the words.* Some words will have to be musically accented. Others might seem like they require a high, low, or sustained note.

6. *Meter*. The lyric's meter and how you read it will help you determine what kind of tempo the song should have.

7. *Blend*. The melody must musically express and complement whatever idea, story, or message the lyric is conveying.

In conclusion, the following might be found helpful when composing a melody to an existing lyric:

1. Read the lyric aloud, emphasizing accents.
2. On a sheet of paper, show accents and rhythmic units.
3. Decide on a time signature.
4. Compose a brief musical idea (motif) from a section of the lyric, paying strict attention to rhythm as well as melody.
5. Develop the motif into a longer musical phrase. The melody may move along the scale, skip to tones within a chord, repeat tones, or move to tones "foreign" to the scale.
6. Develop musical sections from your phrases using repetition and contrast.
7. Experiment with the chords that best enhance the melody and place the chord name above the melody in its proper place on the lead sheet.

The Hook

Common among many songs is a repetitive melody or lyric line referred to as the hook, so called because it literally "hooks" the listener's attention. It is the infectious part of the song that the listener goes away remembering (and often singing) most. The words to it are usually the title of the song, but this doesn't necessarily have to be. A hook can also come in the form of a strong dance beat or rhythmic idea. It is the "catchy" part of the song and is what music publishers, record producers, and artists often look for when auditioning new songs. The top 100 is full of songs with hooks and a glimpse at the charts will reveal those hooks with which you are familiar.

How to Find and Develop Ideas for Melodies

Can you teach a songwriter to be creative? No, but you can teach him ways or ideas on how to be creative. Every songwriter has his own method of finding and developing melodies. A few will be offered here with the hope that you might find one helpful.

1. *Composing from chord progressions.* You might take the chord progression of a favorite song of yours or make up your own chord progression and write a melody around it. (See Appendix B.) Some composers will listen to just the rhythm track of a song, if they have access to one, and write a melody that musically integrates with the harmonies on the track.

2. *Plucking out a melody.* Numerous writers compose simply by "plucking" out notes on the piano or guitar and forming them into a complete song.

3. *Writing from emotion.* Some musical ideas originate and develop out of intense feelings the writer has. How many songs do you think were written out of disheartening love affairs, loneliness, insecurity, parting, or emotions on the opposite scale?

4. *Find a lyric.* Many times trying to set music to a lyric already written out will help. The meaning and meter is already established in the composer's mind, and he can compose a melody from these lyrical suggestions. (Chapter 6 lists magazines which publish popular song lyrics without the music.)

5. *Learn to play a new instrument.* By doing this you might find new chord progressions or pluck out a new melody while attempting to develop your technique.

One of the best ways to develop a melodic idea is to create a hook and build the rest of the song around it. You can do this by making up a short lyrical phrase and then composing a melody for it in your mind. Don't worry about the quality of the melody in the beginning—just sing it over and over to yourself, making whatever changes you feel are necessary to make it good. When you come up with a melody you are satisfied with, play it on a chordal instrument, add harmonies, and then try to expand it into a full-length song.

2: Lead Sheets

A LEAD SHEET is music industry jargon for a musical notation of a song's melody, along with the chord symbols, lyrics, and other pertinent information.

Essentials of the Lead Sheet

A lead sheet is similar to the sheet music you buy in the stores. It contains, essentially, all the same elements, but will usually be a handwritten rather than a printed notation of the notes, chord symbols, and lyric. A lead sheet, of course, will not be offered for commercial sale.

Your lead sheet should contain the following:

1. The song's *title* and the *author*(*s*) of the words and music.

2. *Where you can be reached*—that is, your name, address, and telephone number.

3. *Copyright notice*. Even if you have not filed registration for your song with the Copyright Office, you should write in the proper copyright notice on the first page of your lead sheet (see page 30).

4. The *style* or *tempo* of the music (place this above the first measure of music). This can be "waltz," "slow and rhythmic," "moderately," "with a driving beat," etc.

5. *Treble clef sign*. Lead sheets should be written in the treble clef, the most commonly used clef today. The treble clef sign, or G clef, is written:

6. *Key signature*. The key your song is in should be notated by placing the proper accidentals—flats or sharps (or neither for the key of C)—after the treble clef sign.

7. *Time signature*. Place the time signature on the staff directly after the key signature. The time signature is written to show the method of measuring for your music. A common time signature is $\frac{3}{4}$ ("three-four"). The top number designates how many beats there will be in each measure and the bottom number designates what note value receives one beat. Thus, the $\frac{3}{4}$ time signature specifies that there are 3 beats per measure and the quarter note (or rest) receives one beat.

8. *Bar lines*. Measures are separated by vertical bars or bar lines. The first bar line in the piece is placed after the last note (or rest) of the first measure; that is, *not* after the time signature.

9. *Notes* below the third line should generally have stems going up on the right side; notes on or above the third line should generally have stems going down on the left side:

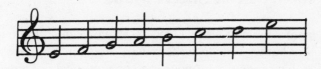

10. *Even spacing*. Space the notes and measures as evenly as possible. Be sure not to crowd sixteenth notes too close together, otherwise you will not be able to fit all the words or syllables that correspond to these notes under the group. Evenly spaced measures make for a more legible and attractive lead sheet copy.

11. *Complete measures*. Each measure must contain the exact combination of note and/or rest values as indicated by the top number of the time signature. This may seem obvious but incomplete measures are found to be a common error.

12. *Lyric*. Write or type the lyric below the musical staff, each

word or syllable directly under the note it corresponds to. For a sustained (tied or whole) note, insert the word or syllable directly under the note and draw a straight line from the bottom of the last letter of the word or syllable to where the next note or rest begins.

13. *Chord symbols.* Write all chord symbols in their proper places above the musical staff—that is, above a particular note, rest, or beat.

All these elements can be observed by examining the lead sheet that appears on pages 18–19.

Never give away your last lead sheet copy. To prevent this, keep your original or master copy in safe keeping. It is advisable that you keep several duplicate copies in a convenient place for easy access when you need them.

It is not always necessary to have a lead sheet when submitting your song to a publisher or producer. If you present a demo (see chapter 3) of a song that they accept, they will assume the responsibility of making one up themselves. But at least have a typed copy of the lyric available.

As its name suggests, a lead sheet guides the person along when listening to your song.

Where to Get Lead Sheets Made

If you are unable to write a lead sheet, you can seek the help of someone who knows how to write music. You can sing, present on tape, or play a presentation of your song on a musical instrument to a music copyist or stenographer, arranger, musician, music teacher, or knowledgeable friend who might be able to write a lead sheet. You will be charged a fee (usually between $8 and $20) for the transcription of the melody onto paper (unless it's a friend, and a good one at that) and the notation of the chord symbols and words.

Professionals can be found in the classified telephone directory under "Music Copyists," "Music Arrangers," "Music Teachers," etc. or in the trades (see chapter 6). A neat manuscript will make the presentation of your song all the more professional.

Reproduction of Your Musical Manuscript

If you have a lead sheet and wish to have copies of it repro-
duced, you can have this done by any of the three basic techniques
for reproducing music manuscripts: diazo process white-print reproduction, photocopying, or photo-offset reproduction.

The following is designed to acquaint you with the advantages
and limitations of each technique.

Diazo Process White-Print Reproduction

This is the most flexible method of reproducing your manuscript. Copies can come in many sizes, be printed on one or both
sides, and be bound in many ways.

The name of this technique comes from the fact that it uses paper
with a special diazo chemical coating. The transparent master copy of
a work is placed in contact with this paper, exposed to ultraviolet
light, and developed in ammonia fumes. Resulting copies from this
technique come out black print on white paper.

Master lead sheets should be made on the most transparent paper
possible. Best results are obtained from 100 percent rag content,
resin-impregnated paper. It should be noted that this is a special kind
of onion-skin paper, referred to as deschon or vellum, and is different
from that sold in stationery stores.

Since the density of the writing on the transparent master effects
the resulting copies, dense, black engrossing ink should be used to
make this copy. Pencils with electro-sensing lead will also make
good copies, but ballpoint or felt-tipped pens will not.

White-print copies can be bound in a few ways. The simplest
method is where the copies with print on one side only are taped
together side by side with transparent tape. (For three or more
sheets, the copies are bound together accordion-style.) White-print
copies with print on both sides can be bound in book form or with a
plastic "spiral" binding. You may wish to assemble several of your
lead sheets together for a song book presentation of your material.
Covers can be added for a more professional appearance.

SAMPLE LEAD SHEET

READY OR NOT (HERE I COME)

MODERATELY, WITH A BEAT

WORDS AND MUSIC BY HARVEY RACHLIN

© 1975 HARVEY RACHLIN

Photocopying

This is the reproduction of copies by photocopying machines. It is often the most convenient method to use because of the availability of photocopying machines and the most economical when only small quantities of a work are needed. Photocopies with print on one side of the paper can be joined with paper tape and be folded accordion-style, while two-sided prints can be punched and bound with a plastic binding. Its major disadvantage, however, is that most photocopying machines can only reproduce copies with a maximum width of 8½ inches.

Photo-Offset Reproduction (Offset Printing)

This is the most economical process to use when many (over five hundred) copies of a work are needed. In photo-offset reproduction, your manuscript is photographed and a printing plate is made from the photographic negative. This plate is then mounted on a rotary press, inked, and the image is printed onto a rubber blanket on the press. Resulting copies printed from the blanket are clear and professional.

For more information and prices on these techniques, consult a music copyist or printer. He can be found in the yellow pages of your telephone directory under "Music Copyist," "Music Manuscript Reproductions," or "Music Printers and Engravers" or in advertisements in the trade magazines.

# 3: Demos

A DEMO, short for demonstration record or tape, is a recording of a song which is used to show its potential to producers, recording artists, record companies, or music publishers for the purpose of having them commercially record or publish the song.

Your aim as a songwriter is to obtain a commercial recording of your song. Unless you can perform your songs live, your demo will be the vehicle to that end. Therefore, you want to have the best, most accurate presentation of your song possible. Many publishers, producers, or artists will tell you to just make a simple recording of your song. The fact is you'll meet many people in the music business who can't "hear" what potential the song has without an elaborate orchestration or arrangement.

Types of Demos

The simplest demo contains a voice accompanied by a chordal instrument (piano or guitar), made on a home cassette or reel-to-reel tape recorder. Make sure the melody and lyrics are clear sounding if you submit such a demo.

A more sophisticated demo might be a rhythm section (piano, bass guitar, lead or rhythm guitar, drums), a lead vocal, and background vocals recorded in a recording studio, usually on either four or eight tracks. (Master recordings contain sixteen or more tracks.) The musicians and vocalists will probably read off a lead sheet. You might even pay to have an "arrangement" made of your song (see chapter 9).

Every attempt should be made to have a "neutral" demo made—that is, a demo that doesn't sound like it's for one particular artist, but best represents the song where it could be recorded by anybody. In this way, you will not lock yourself into the style of any one particular recording artist and your chances for generating wider interest in your song will be increased.

Demo Costs

If you make your demo on a home tape recorder, the only cost you incur is that of the tape, assuming we are not including your original investment for tape machine and microphone.

If you make your demo in a recording studio, then you must pay for recording time, mixing time (in the case of multitrack demos), musician and vocalist fees, and tape costs. Studio rental for mono- or two-track recordings usually range from $20 in the smaller studios to $40 for the larger ones. There are increments in price for the more tracks you use, that is, four- or eight-track recordings. Mixing expenses for multitrack recordings are usually less than the hourly recording rate.

After your song is recorded on tape, you will want to make copies of it to show around. The original tape recording can be copied onto cassettes and reel-to-reel tapes, or be transcribed onto an acetate dub which can cost as low as $3.50 per song or as much as $10 for a stereo acetate recording of one selection. You may request a rate sheet or rate card from the studio where all recording, mixing, and duplication costs will be listed. To find a recording studio, check your classified telephone directory or any of the listings published in the trades.

The fees for musicians and vocalists depend upon whether they are union members or not. If they are, you are obligated to pay them the minimum scale they are entitled to earn under union terms. Such factors as length of time in the studio, how many songs they record, and the number of overdubs they do affect their fee. However, it is found that underscale payments to union members are common for demo recordings even though this is against union regulations.

If the musicians and singers you use are friends, you can negotiate your own scale of payments. Demos do not have to be made by union musicians and vocalists. However, if the demo is ever sold to a record company and released as a master recording, the musicians and singers must be paid in accordance with union terms under master record purchase agreements (see chapter 15). For recording subsequent masters and collecting future residuals, nonunion participants will have to become union members.

There are numerous firms around that specialize in the making of demos. They produce professional sounding demos from lead sheets or home tape recordings at a rate that usually ranges from $8 for a simple demo to $50 for an elaborate one. If you use one of these firms to make your demo, be sure to state any specific requirements you have with regard to your demo, as these are usually mail-order services and you will not be present to voice these requirements when your demo is being made. Demo firms actively advertise their services in the trade magazines.

Presenting Your Demo

Demos can be presented to whomever you are auditioning your song for in any of three ways: reel-to-reel tape, acetate dub, or cassette. Submitting material on cassette is the least recommended for these reasons: the sound is the worst of the three; it is considered the least professional; and many music companies do not have the equipment on which to play cassettes.

Acetate dubs (at 45 or 33⅓ rpm) are acceptable to submit, but the quality considerably lessens after repeated playings. If you decide to submit a dub, be sure to have the title of the song, speed of the record, and your name, address, and telephone number typed onto the label that you adhere to its face. Acetate dubs can be single-faced (grooved on one side) or double-faced (grooved on both sides), therefore containing two selections.

Reel-to-reel tape is the most professional way to submit your songs. Almost all the professional people who will listen to your songs will either have a reel-to-reel tape recorder or access to one. Besides having the best sound, reel-to-reel tape offers other benefits: you can place several songs on the tape (although it is advisable to submit no more than four songs when first presenting your material); the tape can be leadered (songs separated by white tape) for easy access to any selection; and it can be edited if you ever desire. If you decide to leader your tape, be sure to leader in front of the first selection as well as between each song. On the label you adhere to the tape box, type in the tape speed (7½ IPS is best), the selections contained, and your name, address, and telephone number.

Keep a Demo on File

You might find it advantageous to leave a "stock" copy of your song in storage with a recording studio. This will ensure its safe keeping in case you ever lose or accidentally destroy your last copy, and will enable you to quickly obtain a copy of your song by ordering it on the phone if you ever need it in a hurry. In any case, always have a demo on file and be sure never to submit your last copy.

In conclusion, a well-made demo is vital to the future of your song. It is your final word. Make it say exactly what you want.

 **4: Copyrights**

"A COPYRIGHT IS a form of protection given by the law of the United States to the authors of literary, dramatic, musical, artistic and other intellectual works." (Title 17, *U.S. Code*)

Exclusive Rights in Copyrighted Works

The owner of a copyrighted musical composition is granted the following exclusive rights (Section 106, Title 17, *U.S. Code*): *

1. To reproduce the copyrighted work in copies or phonorecords.
2. To prepare derivative works based upon the copyrighted work.
3. To distribute copies or phonorecords of the copyrighted work to the public by sale or other transfer of ownership, or by rental, lease, or lending.
4. To perform the copyrighted work publicly. †
5. To display the copyrighted work publicly.

---

* As stated under the copyright law, effective January 1, 1978.
† Under the law effective until January 1, 1978, the performance right for nondramatic musical compositions is limited to public performances for profit, i.e. *not* public broadcasting, etc.

Who Can Claim a Copyright

1. The author of the work.
2. Anyone to whom the author has assigned his rights of ownership to the copyright.
3. In the cases of a work made for hire, the employer rather than the employee (or creator) is regarded as author for purposes of this title and can claim copyright.

Only those authorized people are permitted to sign the copyright application form.

Copyright application forms may be obtained by written request from the Copyright Office, Library of Congress, Washington, D.C. 20559, or by telephone (703–557–8700).

United States Copyright Law

On October 19, 1976, President Gerald R. Ford signed into law a broad, new, and long-overdue revision of United States copyright legislation. Copyright Revision Bill S. 22 became Public Law 94-553 and is the first completely new copyright law since 1909. It took 21 years for Congress to approve this modern copyright law, as it began in 1955 to undertake revision.

Several items in the new law affect the songwriter and publisher, and as Barbara Ringer, the U.S. Register of Copyrights said, the new law "comes down on the authors' and creators' side in almost every instance." Except for particular exceptions, all provisions of the new statute enter into force starting January 1, 1978, and supersede the Copyright Act of 1909, as amended, which remains in force until the new enactment takes effect.

The following items from the new law are of importance to the songwriter and music publisher:

Single National Copyright System

The new law establishes a single national system of statutory protection for all copyrightable works, whether published or unpublished. Common law, which gives a work protection under the common laws of the various states before it is published, will be superseded by the single national system effective January 1, 1978.

Duration of Copyright

For works under statutory protection before January 1, 1978, the new law retains the first term of copyright of 28 years from first publication (or from registration in some cases), renewable by certain persons for a second period of protection, but it increases the length of the second period by 19 years for a total term of 47 years. Copyrights in their first term prior to January 1, 1978, must still be renewed to receive the full new maximum term of 75 years, but copyrights in their second term, between December 31, 1976, and December 31, 1977, are automatically extended up to the maximum of 75 years without the need for further renewal.

For works created after January 1, 1978, the new law provides for a term lasting for the author's life plus an additional 50 years after the author's death. If there is joint authorship, the term is for life plus an additional 50 years with respect to the last author to survive. For works made for hire and for anonymous and pseudonymous works (unless the author's identity is revealed in Copyright Office records), the new term will be 75 years from publication or 100 years from creation, whichever is shorter.

For unpublished works that are already in existence on January 1, 1978, but that are not protected by statutory copyright and have not yet gone into the public domain, the new law will generally provide automatic federal copyright protection for the same life-plus-fifty or 75/100-year terms prescribed for new works. Special dates of termination are provided for copyrights in older works of this sort.

The new law does not restore copyright protection for any work that has gone into the public domain.

Termination of Transfers

Under the 1909 copyright law, after the first term of 28 years, the renewal copyright reverts in certain situations to the author or other specified beneficiaries. The new law drops the renewal feature except for works already in their first term of statutory protection when the new law becomes effective. Instead, for transfers of rights made by an author or certain of the author's heirs after January 1, 1978, the new law generally permits the author or certain heirs to terminate the transfer after 35 years by serving written notice on the transferee within specified time limits.

For those existing works which a songwriter has assigned the renewal term of copyright to a publisher, the new law provides a procedure by which, upon giving specifically required notices, the writer can have the renewal rights revested in him for 19 years. This provision was designed to give those songwriters who assigned away their entire copyrights the benefit of the new law's extended term, since existing works in their original term will be granted a total period of 75 years of protection if renewal is properly applied for. Those works already in renewal will be equalized by allowing the creator to renegotiate or remove altogether from his publisher the 19 years of protection he would have additionally received had the copyright still been in its first term.

Compulsory Royalty Rate for Recordings

With respect to the compulsory licensing for recordings of music, the new law raises the statutory royalty from 2 cents to a rate of 2.75 cents or one-half cent per minute of playing time, whichever amount is larger.

New Compulsory License Fees

Copyright owners receive under the new law revenue from three sources which previously have not paid a compulsory license fee. The three new sources are public broadcasting entities, cable television systems, and jukebox operators.

Copyright Royalty Tribunal

The new law creates a Copyright Royalty Tribunal whose purpose will be to determine whether copyright royalty rates, in such categories as sound recordings, public broadcasting entities, cable television systems, and jukeboxes, are reasonable and, if not, to adjust them.

Copyright Registration Fee

The fee to be paid to the Register of Copyrights for the registration of a copyright claim to a published or unpublished work, including the issuance of a certificate of registration, will be increased from

$6 to $10. (Note: This does not include registration fees for such categories as renewal registrations, notice of intention to make phonorecords, recordation of assignments, etc.)

Statutory Registration of Unpublished Lyrics
    The new law permits copyright registration for unpublished lyrics or song poems. Under the law, in effect until December 31, 1977, unpublished lyrics, without music, may not be registered for copyright protection.

Deposit of Copies
    For purposes of copyright registration of musical works, the new law allows for one complete copy or phonorecord of an unpublished work to be submitted. For a published work, two complete copies or phonorecords of the best edition of the work must be submitted.

Notice of Copyright
    The new law calls for published copies of music to contain the notice of copyright. However, omission or errors in the notice of copyright will not immediately result in the copyright's becoming public domain. Violators will have a certain time period within which to correct omissions or errors.

Copyrighting Musical Compositions

    To register your claim for copyright registration of an unpublished work, complete and sign Form E,* submit one complete copy (lead sheet) of your song, and the proper statutory fee, payable to the Register of Copyrights, and send these three items to: Copyright Office, Library of Congress, Washington, D.C. 20559.
    Do *not* send the only copy of your work for copyright registration. The Copyright Office does not return your submitted copy. When your work has been registered, the Copyright Office will return

---

* Subject to change by the Copyright Office effective January 1, 1978.

to you within five to ten weeks half of the copyright registration form with the copyright seal embossed on it and a registration number printed on it as evidence that your claim has been registered.

When your song is published, the copyright proprietor will repeat this procedure but will submit two copies of the best edition of the work as first published with the copyright notice. If your song has been previously registered, the publisher, if other than yourself, will request that you assign your copyright to him, and will thereafter register such assignment of copyright form with the Copyright Office. To renew a copyright (applicable only to works registered prior to January 1, 1978) a renewal form with the statutory fee must be received by the Copyright Office by the last day of the twenty-eighth year of the original term of copyright. Failure to file within the prescribed limit results in the work going into the public domain.

The Copyright Notice

The copyright notice should appear on all copies of your songs. Three elements are contained in the notice:

1. The symbol © (the letter C in a circle), the word "Copyright," or the abbreviation "Copr."
2. The year the song has been registered for copyright or if published, the year of first publication of the work and year date of registration for the unpublished version.
3. The copyright owner's name.

The copyright notice looks like this: © 1977 Johnny Songwriter.

You should place the copyright notice on the title page or first page of music. Even if your song has not been registered with the Copyright Office, this notice should appear on all copies of your lead sheets or sheet music when you begin circulating it to indicate your rights when copies of your work are distributed beyond your control.

Copyright Registration of Unpublished Song Collections

For those songwriters who are constantly turning out a lot of tunes and find the copyright registration costs too expensive, they may register two or more unpublished compositions with a single application and fee.

This consists of assembling all your songs in a neat, orderly fashion. The collection will bear a single title that must be listed in the proper space provided for on the copyright application form. The collection in its entirety is the subject of a single copyright claim. (Be sure to keep a copy of each song in the collection on file.) When you wish to have an individual song from your collection catalogued and indexed under its own title, it will be necessary for you to register it separately.

Copyright Infringement of Musical Compositions

A copyright registration certificate is no guarantee of originality of a song. It is simply evidence that approximates a date of the song's creation. Such information and registration certificate is necessary if one wishes to bring a lawsuit against an alleged infringer of his composition in federal court. A lawsuit in federal court as opposed to state court provides for stipulated damages and in certain circumstances will provide for tripling those damages.

Before January 1, 1978, an original work which has not been published is protected under the common law without the necessity of filing a claim to copyright. In the event an infringement occurs regarding a composition which has not been registered under federal statute, one would bring a lawsuit in the state court under common law.

To prove plagiarism or copyright infringement of a song, one must prove *substantial similarity* between the two songs and that the alleged copier had *access* to the song. Copyright infringement cases involving musical compositions deal first with similarity. Substantial similarity between the two songs brings up the possibility of an infringement. Despite popular misconception, there is no rigid standard for the number of duplicate bars which will constitute an infringement. Courts have previously ruled two duplicate bars to be sufficient in a particular set of circumstances and as many as six to be insufficient. If, however, substantial similarity is found, then the element of "access" must be examined. Did the alleged copier have access to the song? Access may include anything from seeing a lead sheet of the song or hearing it played privately to hearing it played on the radio.

As always, the advice of an attorney specializing in music or entertainment law, henceforth referred to in this book as a "music attorney," is highly recommended for any questions you have regarding this (or any other) area of law. If you don't know of any, you may find one by calling the referral service of your local or state bar association.

Copyrighting Sound Recordings

The 1909 Copyright Law was amended to provide copyright protection for any sound recording made after February 15, 1972. This affords record companies and music publishers legal protection against those who pirate their product.

The copyright law defines sound recordings as "works that result from the fixation of a series of musical, spoken, or other sounds, but not including the sounds accompanying a motion picture or other audiovisual work, regardless of the nature of the material objects, such as disks, tapes, or other phonorecords, in which they are embodied." * Common examples of reproductions of sound recordings include phonograph records, reel-to-reel tapes, cassettes, eight-track tapes, and player piano rolls.

The record company issuing your song, or, if you have formed your own record company and are releasing a sound recording, must properly file Form N * with the Copyright Office. The Copyright Office registers only published sound recordings.†

To secure statutory copyright in a sound recording you must:

---

* Subject to change by the Copyright Office effective January 1, 1978.
† This requirement (that the sound recording must be published) is subject to change under the new law.

> *First:* Produce copies that include the copyright notice. To
> secure copyright, reproductions of the sound recording must
> bear the copyright notice in the required form and position,
> as explained below.
>
> *Second:* Publish * the sound recording with the copyright no-
> tice. The date of publication is the earliest date which copies
> were placed on sale, sold, or publicly distributed by the
> copyright owner or those under his authority.
>
> *Third:* Register your claim to copyright. After publication,
> promptly mail to the Register of Copyrights, Library of Con-
> gress, Washington, D.C. 20559, two copies of the best edi-
> tion of the sound recording as first published with the copy-
> right notice, application Form N † properly completed, and
> the statutory fee.

The copyright notice for sound recordings should appear on the
surface of the copy in such a manner and location that reasonable
notice of the claim to copyright is given.

Three elements are contained in this notice:

1. the symbol ℗
2. the year of first publication
3. the copyright owner's name.

Example: ℗ 1977 John Doe Records, Inc.

Notice of Use of Copyrighted Music on Mechanical Instruments **

Copyright Office Circular 51 says: ''This form should be filed
by the owner of copyright in a musical composition when he has
recorded his work or licensed it for recording on mechanical instruments such as phonograph records.''

The owner of a copyright has the exclusive right, under copyright law, to make the first recording or reproduction of his musical

---

* This requirement (that the sound recording must be published) is subject to change under
the new law.
† Subject to change by the Copyright Office effective January 1, 1978.
** Effective January 1, 1978, the ''Notice of Use'' will no longer be required to be filed with the
Copyright Office.

work on mechanical devices such as phonograph records or tape recordings. After the copyright owner has permitted the composition to be recorded, other persons, under certain conditions, have the right to make a recording of the work. Such persons may either negotiate a recording contract for the copyright owner's composition to be recorded under specified terms in the agreement or they may use the "compulsory license" provisions of the law to use the copyright owner's song (see chapter 11) which do not require them to get permission from the copyright owner.

Under the 1909 Copyright Law, at the time the copyright owner has recorded his work or licensed another person to make the first recording, he is required to file a "Notice of Use" (Form U) with the Copyright Office. Failure to file "Notice of Use" can result in another record company releasing the copyright owner's song without paying him mechanical royalties.

Under the new copyright law, the filing of "Notice of Use" by the copyright owner will no longer be required. Instead, the person who wants the compulsory license must within thirty days after making, and before distributing, any phonorecords of the work, serve a notice of intention to do so on the copyright owner. If the registration or public records of the Copyright Office do not identify the copyright owner by name and address, the seeker of the compulsory license can file his notice of intention in the Copyright Office instead. To be entitled to receive royalties under a compulsory license, the copyright owner must be identified in the registration or other public records of the Copyright Office.

Failure by the person seeking the compulsory license to serve or file a notice of intention forecloses the possibility of a compulsory license and, in the absence of a negotiated license, renders the making and distribution of phonorecords actionable as acts of infringement.

5: How to Get Your Songs Commercially Recorded

IN ORDER TO GET your songs commercially recorded, you will be auditioning them with various music business personnel who are in a position to either place your songs with the proper people to get them recorded or accept it for commercial recording themselves.

You will be submitting your material to any of the following: music publisher, record producer, record company, recording artist, manager, booking agent, a "contact" of yours. The audition will take place in either one of two ways: you will be present when your songs are being auditioned, or you will mail or drop off your material to be heard at the listener's convenience. It is advisable to have each song you audition copyrighted before submission.

Your songs will be auditioned by a demo or by live performance. In either case, have a lead sheet or a typed lyric sheet ready to give to the listener before playing your material.

Before you begin to place your songs, you must decide what area of the commercial music market your songs belong to, who are the active individuals and companies within that market, and where to reach them. Finding the answers to these questions will involve preparation on your behalf.

Determining Your Song's Classification

You must first determine to which category or categories of commercial music your song belongs. You will obviously not, for instance, pursue a country and western recording artist, publisher, or record producer with a rhythm and blues tune, but you should be creative in determining which artists within your song's category might be suitable to record it. Very often an artist will make modifications in his or her style, or, as in the case of older recording artists, look for contemporary material so they may broaden their commercial appeal.

Reaching the Proper People

After you have determined your song's classification, you are ready to begin your homework. You must determine to whom to bring your song and where to reach them.

The best sources of information for names, addresses, and telephone numbers of music publishers, record producers, record companies, recording artists, managers, booking agents, and other music business personnel are the trades and various other music publications listed in chapter 6.

A very prominent and successful music publisher was once asked how he goes about getting the songs in his catalog recorded. He said he reviews the singles charts in the trades in the category for which his song might be appropriate. (The trades have separate top 100 charts for pop, soul, and country and western records.) He then notes every artist or record producer (this information is given) who might be suitable to record the particular song he is working on, and after finding where to reach them, he auditions it either by personal appointment or by mail.

If you can get your material directly to a recording artist or record producer, you might fare better than by sending it to the music publisher who in turn often auditions it for these same people. The fact that the publishing rights to your song are available might add more weight to it for the artist or producer interested in acquiring these rights.

If you are a singer-songwriter, the following course of action is recommended for you. Make a good demo of about three or four of your best songs. This means hiring a few musicians (no more than a rhythm section) and going into a studio (or use a good home machine) to record your material. No fancy production in the studio is necessary. Simply make a demo that brings out the best of you as a singer and the best in your songs.

Then make an appointment with an A & R director or independent producer (see chapter 8). If they like your material and decide to work with you, they will either use your demo and "sweeten" it (to release as a master) or rerecord your song as a master with you as the artist and an arrangement and production that best befits both.

Music publishers often sign singer-songwriters and make deals with record labels for them, while, of course, retaining the publishing interests. If the publisher gets you a label deal, he will sign you to an exclusive songwriter's contract. (Many provisions you should attempt to have included in your contract appear in chapter 13.)

Singer-songwriters are at a great advantage today. Not only because they can sing their own demos and tailor them just as they want but also because publishers, producers, and record companies actively seek such a talent. More groups and individual singers are self-contained today than ever before. As a matter of fact, whereas self-contained artists were the exception in the past, they are fast becoming the rule today, and the exception to the trend is the artist who seeks outside material.

Auditioning Your Songs

Appointments

You should always try to be present when your songs are being auditioned. If your material is rejected, you will find out why and probably even receive suggestions on how to improve it. If your songs are borderline, you can ask for permission to resubmit them after the proper improvements are made. In any case, your songs will receive more personal attention and by auditioning your songs live, a certain rapport (hopefully for the better!) will be established

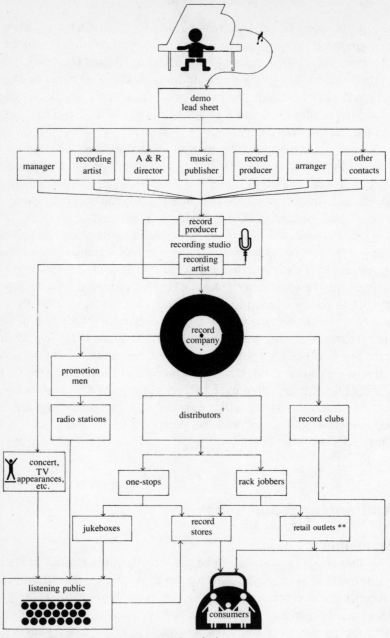

Tracing the Pathway of a Song

* pressing plant (owned by record company or independent)
† record company owned "branches" or independent ("indie") distributors
** department stores, discount stores, drugstores, variety stores, supermarkets

between you and the listener. You might be invited to come back at a later date to "pitch" more songs.

The music business, more than most, is built on personal relationships with people. By developing and maintaining personal contact with people in the business, you will get to know what type of material they are looking for and even how they will react when listening to new material of yours. And, of course, their door will always be open for you to bring them more songs.

The majority of music business activity takes place at a few established music centers. These are in New York, Los Angeles, and Nashville plus the many small but important ones cropping up all the time. Visiting one of these music centers might prove beneficial for developing new contacts and getting your songs recorded.

Mailing Your Songs

Before mailing your songs, it is advisable for you to ask for permission to do so first. Many companies will not accept unsolicited material through the mail. (Also find out if they will accept your songs if sent by registered mail, as it is advisable to send your material this way.) After receiving permission, send a demo of your song with a lead sheet or typed lyric sheet and a self-addressed stamped envelope. Again, it is highly recommended the material you mail be copyrighted before submission.

Never send just a lead sheet of your song for evaluation or audition purposes. Professionals in the music business often cannot read music or if they can, might interpret it differently from what you conceived. Lyric sheets should not be sent alone either. Professionals want to hear a complete song, not just read a lyric.

Follow Up Your Song's Audition

After you have auditioned your song by appointment or by mail, it is a good idea for you to follow up the audition with a brief thank-you note, or phone call, which will help keep your identity fresh in the listener's memory and may also serve as a means for developing a personal rapport with him.

If you mailed your songs and haven't received any response

after a certain time period (a month is adequate), write or call the publisher to inquire as to the status of your material.

Other Methods for Getting Your Songs Commercially Recorded

To get your songs recorded, they must first have exposure. You do not necessarily have to audition them with people who are affiliated with a music company. There are alternatives and you should actively pursue these if you have not had success with music business personnel in the manner previously discussed. As a matter of fact, these methods have often been successfully used as a first approach to getting songs recorded or by songwriters who live far from the mainstream of music industry activity.

Radio stations. Many local radio stations will play (and plug) a local denizen's material. If enough interest in a song is generated, someone connected with the music business, as for instance, a local record distributor, may be contacted, who in turn might put the songwriter in contact with people who can get his song moving. Make an appointment with the station's music director or one of the station's DJs to audition your material for airplay.

Local talent. Your hometown might very well have some young, aspiring talent wishing to make his or her way to the top. Perhaps your songs might place that person in the right direction. Visit local clubs and contact any singer or group that might be suitable to sing your songs. The right person singing the right song invites success.

Showcases. Many nightclubs sponsor showcases to expose unknown talent. Some designate one night a week expressly for this purpose. Since booking agents and talent scouts frequent such events, it might be wise for you or someone who can perform your music to do so. Don't overlook the fact that many record companies and music publishers are continually on the lookout for new talent and sponsor showcases themselves. Read the trades to find out when these occur.

Songwriters' Agents

A songwriter normally does not work with an agent for the purpose of exploiting his musical composition; that is the function of the music publisher. Once a writer assigns his copyright to the publisher, however, the publisher exploits the work in the capacity of trustee to the copyright rather than the writer's agent.

If a songwriter is also a recording artist he may work through an agent to secure work as a performer. Songwriters whose specialty is to compose music for motion pictures and television, which music is normally written under "employee-for-hire" agreements, will use agents to secure employment and to negotiate such agreements.

In many instances, attorneys who are involved in their songwriter clients' careers have relationships with such clients that go beyond servicing their legal needs and very often perform tasks which might otherwise be performed by agents.

6: Keeping Up with the Trades and Other Music Publications

ONE OF THE MOST important factors in the songwriter's pursuit of success is whether he is informed of what's happening in the music business. This includes knowing which songs are making the charts, who the artists, producers, and publishers of these songs are, which new artists are singing with what labels, what new companies are being formed, who the new and rising executives are, and who is looking for material.

The greatest source of this information can be found in the trades—publications reporting the news of the music business (*Billboard, Cash Box,* and *Record World*). Publishers, record companies, artists, producers, agents, and managers all read at least one of these magazines weekly. How else could they keep abreast of all the activities in the music business when there is so much going on all the time? Without the knowledge of these ''current events'' they are sure to lag behind the competition.

As a songwriter, you can take advantage of the trades by reading them wisely and following up on all leads and information given. The top 100 singles lists, for example, are a wealth of information in themselves. The publishers and producers for these songs are listed, and contacting them to audition your songs should be high on your priority list.

No songwriting book or manual can better inform the songwriter of music industry activities and trends than the trades and other related publications. It cannot be overemphasized how important it is for the songwriter to read these and stay informed. This education process is a never-ending one, and is imperative for success.

Music Industry Trades

Billboard (1 Astor Plaza, 1515 Broadway, New York, New York 10036) is published weekly and available at some newsstands or by subscription. *Billboard* also publishes special supplements that are invaluable for the songwriter. These include: *Billboard International Buyer's Guide*—a comprehensive listing of domestic and foreign music publishers, record companies, record producers, music organizations, sheet music jobbers, record and tape wholesalers, record pressers, record accessory and supply manufacturers and jukebox manufacturers, with their addresses and phone numbers (published yearly and is free for subscribers); *Billboard's Annual Campus Attractions*—a supplement containing the names of recording artists, the labels they record for, their personal managers and booking agents, and their addresses and phone numbers (free for subscribers); and *Billboard's Annual World of Country Music*—includes lists of the top country songs, labels, music publishers, news of the country music scene and listings of country artists, their personal managers and booking agents, and their addresses and phone numbers (free for subscribers).

Billboard also publishes sourcebooks for the disco and country music fields, and a recording studio and equipment directory. These supplements are sent free to subscribers. In their annual magazine issue they publish lists of the top songs, artists, record producers, music publishers, and record companies for the year.

Cash Box (119 West 57th Street, New York, New York 10019) is published weekly and available at some newsstands or by subscription. *Cash Box* also publishes an annual directory.

Record World (1700 Broadway, New York, New York 10019) is published weekly and available at some newsstands or by subscription. *Record World* also publishes an annual directory.

The following is a list of other trade and music publications the songwriter might find invaluable.

Songwriter Publications

Songwriter's Review (1697 Broadway, New York, New York 10019) is the oldest songwriters' publication still in existence. Established in 1946 and published every two months, *Songwriter's Review* carries feature articles of interest to the songwriter as well as useful trade information, tips, and advice. *Songwriter's Review* also publishes an annual directory listing ASCAP, BMI, and SESAC music publishers, major labels, disc distributors, record producers, artists and their managers, and music organizations. Heavy advertisements include demo firms, songwriting books and aids, and collaboration services. The magazine is available by subscription only.

Songwriter Magazine (P.O. Box 3510, Hollywood, California 90028). The first issue premiered in October 1975, and this magazine will undoubtedly be around for a long time to come. Features include interviews, information on which music publishers are seeking material, chart listings, and music news. It is published monthly and available by subscription or at some newsstands.

New on the Charts (Music Business Reference, 1500 Broadway, New York, New York 10036) is an invaluable publication for music publishers and songwriters. It lists the songs, artists, producers, publishers, and record labels making the charts and their addresses and phone numbers, as well as the artists' managers and booking agents. It is cross-referenced by each of the above for quick derivation of the information (published monthly and available by subscription only).

Tunesmith (P.O. Box 3839, Hollywood, California 90028) is a monthly newsletter that tells which artists, producers, and publishers are looking for material. Their addresses are included as well as an analysis of the charts. It covers the pop, rhythm and blues, country and western, and easy listening fields. Available by subscription only.

Music-related Publications

The following publications contain trade news and other information the songwriter might find useful:

Official Talent and Booking Directory (P.O. Box 3030, Los Angeles, California 90028) lists most U.S. popular recording artists, their managers and booking agents, as well as the latter's addresses and telephone numbers.

Variety (154 West 46th Street, New York, New York 10036) is a weekly entertainment newspaper that contains news on show business, including the latest in the music field.

Musician's Guide (739 Boylston Street, Boston, Massachusetts 02116) is a monthly magazine that contains information of interest for today's musician, including at least one article per issue on songwriting.

Song Hits (Charlton Publications, Charlton Building, Derby, Connecticut 06418) is a monthly magazine that prints the lyrics to the latest pop, soul, and country and western hits.

Hit Parader (Charlton Publications, Charlton Building, Derby, Connecticut 06418) is a monthly magazine containing news of the top recording artists, record reviews, and lyrics to the most successful rock songs.

Rolling Stone (745 Fifth Avenue, New York, New York 10019) is a weekly newspaper containing interviews and the latest news in the music business.

Filmusic Notebook (P.O. Box 261, Calabasa, California 91302) is a nifty little publication for all those interested in motion picture music. It is not really a trade magazine in the sense the others are, but it is packed with information about film music. Includes interviews with the greatest motion picture composers of all time and soundtrack albums to motion pictures not ordinarily found in retail stores; available for purchase by subscribers.

Downbeat (222 W. Adams Street, Chicago, Illinois 60606) (biweekly)

Sing Out! (270 Lafayette Street, New York, New York 10012) (bimonthly)

The Hollywood Reporter (6715 Sunset Blvd. Hollywood, California 90028) (daily)

Melody Maker (24–34 Meymott Street, London SE1 9LU, England) (weekly)

High Fidelity/Backbeat (The Publishing House, Great Barrington, Massachusetts 01230) (monthly)

Country Music Magazines

Country Song Roundup
Charlton Publications
Charlton Building
Derby, Connecticut 06418
(monthly)

Nashville Sound
Charlton Publications
Charlton Building
Derby, Connecticut 06418
(bimonthly)

Country Music Magazine
P.O. Box 2560
Boulder, Colorado 80322
(monthly)

Country Style
11058 W. Addison St.
Franklin Park, Illinois 60131
(monthly)

Country Rambler
P.O. Box 1080
Skokie, Illinois 60076
(bimonthly)

7: The Music Publisher

A MUSIC PUBLISHER is the person or company who 1) screens songs and attempts to get them commercially recorded, 2) exploits the copyright, 3) protects the copyright, and 4) collects income from all sources. A musical copyright has four separate sources: performance, mechanical, synchronization, and printing.

Types of Music Publishers

Music publishers range in size from one-man operations to large corporations and run the gamut to include firms that publish any kind of music to those which specialize in one particular type.

A further division of music publishing companies can be made upon close examination of this market. There are independent publishing companies who are involved full time in exploiting the copyrights (causing the songs to be used to derive their maximum potential income) in their catalog, publishing companies formed by record labels to publish songs recorded by their artists, and companies formed because the producer or artist of a record has acquired a piece or all of the publishing rights to the song being recorded. This last type of publisher will usually have a larger, more experienced firm administrate his catalog. This is because his creative activities prevent them from devoting the necessary time to copyright and financial administration, but nonetheless, welcome the chance to publish songs as it adds to their income. Because the producer or artist is in such a strong position to determine whether or not a song will be recorded, songwriters may hear them say something like, "If you want your song recorded, we require such and such percentage of the publishing."

The Role of the Music Publisher

1. *Screens new material*. Many publishing companies have on staff a person called the "professional manager." His job is to screen all new material that comes into the office, to seek out potential hit songs from other sources, and then try to get them recorded by contacting producers, artists, A & R directors, or whatever contact he has that can aid him in getting a song commercially recorded. The professional manager is the person at the publishing company you want to see. You should always try to get a personal appointment with him, but there will be cases where if you want a particular publisher to hear your song you will have to mail it in (see page 39).

If a publisher accepts your song, he will use your demo if it is a good representation of it; otherwise, he will hire musicians and vocalists to go into a recording studio and cut a demo. The publisher will offer you a contract when he accepts your song. It is recommended you consult a music attorney before signing. Contracts may vary from publisher to publisher, but you, the songwriter, should have certain basic rights. (Some of these are outlined in chapter 13.)

2. *Exploits the copyright*. The publisher will take the song to anybody who might record it and audition it for that person. He will study the charts, see which artists and producers are hitting, and attempt to get them to hear it. If the song does get recorded and released, the publisher often helps promote the song along with the record company. He might help to get airplay or advertise the song in any form of the media.

Many artists will record a song previously recorded. Such a version is called a "cover record." The publisher will attempt to get every artist whose style is compatible to the song to record it. The goal of every publisher is to make his song a standard.

The publisher will also try to subpublish the song—that is, have a foreign publisher (referred to as the subpublisher) get the song represented and recorded in his territory. The standard contract for this calls for the subpublisher to pay the United States publisher (referred to as the original publisher) 50 percent of all income he collects from the song. The exception to this is with regard to printed editions sold in the foreign territory for which the subpublisher pays the United States publisher a smaller percentage of royalties earned on such editions.

All net foreign income the United States publisher receives is split equally with the songwriter except for those moneys collected from the performing rights organization (see chapter 10). The songwriter receives his share of such royalty directly from his performing rights organization and it is usually 50 percent of the total performance royalties earned in the particular country, except in cases where foreign lyrics were written, in which case the writer of those lyrics normally would receive 25 percent of the total writer's share of the territorial performance income.

The music publisher is unlike any other type of publisher. With the creation of the phonograph record, music publishers found another source of revenue—mechanical income. The development of modern technology has added other sources of income for the music publisher and songwriter, such as that from tapes, films, and various electrical transcriptions. Since the music publisher acts in so many capacities for popularizing a songwriter's material, he has also been popularly referred to as a songwriter's agent, although this is technically inaccurate.

3. *Protects the copyright.* Once your song has been recorded and released, certain registration forms and copies of the song must be filed with the Copyright Office. It is up to the publisher to see that these are properly filed.

The publisher also sees that the copyright is protected from illegal exploitation. He will take action against those who pirate (unauthorized reproduction and selling of records and tapes) or bootleg (unauthorized recording and selling of a performance of the song) the record. He will also notify the songwriter when the copyright is up for renewal and may renegotiate a contract for its second or extended term of copyright for works copyrighted prior to January 1, 1978.

4. *Collects and distributes copyright income.* If your song gets commercially recorded, the usual agreement is that you and the publisher share all the revenues the song generates equally—50 percent to the songwriter and 50 percent to the publisher, except for income from printed editions of the music which is a negotiable contract term that calls for a specified amount per copy of sheet music sold or a percentage of the retail selling price of copies sold to be paid to the songwriter by the publisher and is almost always less than the latter's share.

There are four sources of income for a song: performance royalties, mechanical royalties, synchronization income, and income from printed editions of the song.

Performance royalties are those moneys earned from the use of a song on radio, television, wired music and other similar services. The amount of performance money you earn from use of your song depends primarily upon how often your song is performed and in which particular medium. Performing rights organizations collect license fees from users of music and distribute them to songwriters and publishers (see chapter 10). Under the new law, performances of songs on cable television, public broadcasting entities, and jukeboxes will generate new revenue for the copyright owners of the performed works.

Mechanical royalties, essentially, are those moneys earned for each record or tape of the song sold. There are mechanical rights organizations whose purpose is to collect these royalties and distribute them to their publisher affiliates who in turn pay the songwriter his share of the royalty (see chapter 11).

A television producer or motion picture company may wish to use your song in a taped television show or motion picture they are making. The music publisher, or its mechanical rights organization when authorized to do so, will issue them a *synchronization* license for a negotiated fee which gives them the right to use the copyright in synchronization (timed-relation) to their tape or film.* Copyright owners also receive performance royalties from European theatrical exhibitions of films containing their music (see chapter 17).

---

* Effective January 1, 1978, public broadcasting entities in addition to having to pay for performance licenses will have to pay synchronization license fees to the copyright owners for use of their copyrights.

The publisher will see to it that once the song has achieved a certain degree of success, it is made available in printed editions and properly distributed to retail outlets for public purchase (*printed editions royalties*). This includes use of the copyright in sheet music, songbooks, folios, and stage and marching band arrangements. Songwriters earn a percentage of the retail selling price of each copy of sheet music sold in the United States and Canada containing their copyright. Payment for use of a song in songbooks and folios is either a one-time fixed sum or a percentage of the retail selling price of editions sold containing the copyright.

The publisher will exploit the song both here and abroad and collect from all sources the income he is entitled to. When the publisher pays the songwriter his royalties, he does not withhold any tax. It is important, therefore, that the songwriter properly appropriate part of his income for this purpose. The songwriter should be able to evaluate his correct taxes from the semiannual royalty statements the publisher provides.

Many of the larger music publishing companies hire staff writers. All amateur songwriters would like the chance to staff-write for a music publisher, but chances are they won't unless they show great potential, the company is interested in several of their tunes, or the songwriter has had some commercial success. If you are offered such a contract, give your exclusive songwriter's contract careful consideration before signing (see chapter 13).

8: The Record Producer

THE RECORD PRODUCER is the person who supervises all aspects in the making of a record and is responsible for its outcome. His job includes finding and matching the right song with the right artist, securing the right arrangement, musicians, engineer, studio sound, and finally mixing (blending) all the tracks into the final recording released to the public. The producer also watches the recording expenses to make sure they don't exceed his allotted budget.

Types of Record Producers

Producers may be categorized into two types:

1. *Staff producers*—individuals hired exclusively by a record company to produce one or more artists signed to their label. Staff producers sometimes fulfill certain other capacities in addition to that of record production for the company and are referred to as A & R directors (see page 54).

2. *Independent record producers*—free-lancers who may be: a) signed to a production agreement with a label to produce one or more of the company's artists. These producers are free to make production agreements with as many different record companies as they wish. The production agreement with a company may, in addition, require the producer to supply a certain number of masters within a specified

time period with the right to produce unaffiliated recording artists of his own choosing. b) A member of a musical group who produces the group and is affiliated with a record company in an artist-label relationship but not signed to the label as a staff producer. c) An individual who produces a master with the goal of selling it to a record company. Due to the keen competition that exists today, producing a master in advance to a production agreement can be risky business. But because it can result in great profits, it has become common practice for individuals who would not normally assume this capacity to do so (see chapter 15).

Production Deals

If a record company decides to acquire a master from a producer not previously contracted to make it, it may procure the master in one of the following ways: The company might reimburse the producer for the cost of the recording sessions and offer him a production royalty on all records sold; the company might in addition to session reimbursements and production royalties offer the producer a certain sum of money; the company might contract the record on a royalty basis only without reimbursing the producer for recording costs.

Royalties for record producers are based on a percentage of the retail list price of 90 percent of all records manufactured and sold. This percentage is determined in negotiations between the producer and the record company and usually ranges from 7 to 10 percent, from which the producer must pay the artist his royalty. It is not unusual, however, for successful producers to obtain more than 10 percentage points. It is standard practice for all moneys paid in advance to the producer to be deducted from future earnings of that record.

The Enterprising Record Producer

Record producers are often songwriters, arrangers, and musicians as well. Because many producers recognize the growth potential from their talents, they form all-in-one companies—a conglomerate that includes publishing, management, and booking as well as production. Some producers even have their own record company, affiliated with a larger one to handle their distribution and promotion.

Many songwriters envision themselves in this all-encompassing position. They want to grow beyond their stature as a writer to include it all: producer, arranger, publisher, talent scout, record company. Many individuals have realized this dream not only for the obvious financial rewards but for the satisfying results they may professionally feel.

The producer who is signed to a label or to a recording artist is the ideal candidate for the songwriter to audition his songs. Because the producer has such a great amount of influence on which songs will be recorded, both songwriters and publishers constantly compete for the producer's acceptance of their songs. Building a good personal relationship with a producer might influence his decision to record your song. Many publishing firms wine and dine them for this very reason. It is apparent that a system of "politics" can play an important role in the selection process, but such is the woe of not just the music business, but many others as well.

You should contact producers to audition your songs. Next to the recording artist, they are the hardest group to find an address or telephone number for. If you would like to submit a song to the producer of a particular recording artist, find out his name by checking the production credits on that artist's album or single. You can then try to obtain the producer's address by contacting the record label or from any of the sources described in chapter 6.

The record producer can be your ticket into the music business.

The A & R Director

As noted earlier, record companies have a person in charge of auditioning new artists, songs for the company's artists, and master records. These personnel are referred to as artists and repertoire

(A & R) directors. In addition to these duties, the A & R director often produces one or more artists signed to the company.

The A & R director's job hinges on his ability to pick hits and his job performance is easy to evaluate. How many records is the company selling? How many chart songs does the label have? This position has one of the highest turnovers of any job in the music business. You may spend months building a personal relationship with one or find an A & R director willing to record your material, only to soon find out he has been canned.

You should make an appointment with the A & R director when you want to have your songs auditioned for one of his company's artists (sometimes, he may turn your material down even if it is good, only because he does not see it as fitting the style of his label's artists); when you are a singer-songwriter and are interested in having yourself signed to the label as an artist as well (see chapter 5); you have produced a master and wish to sell it to the label.

Getting an appointment with an A & R director can be difficult because of his busy work schedule, which includes considerable traveling and time devoted for scouting new talent. But you should be persistent in your efforts to reach him personally because mailing your tape in may only result in its getting lost at the bottom of one of the many piles in his office.

Other responsibilities of the A & R director include doing paperwork with regard to record licenses once his company receives an artist's masters; overseeing the completion of the album with regard to artwork, album design, and liner notes; overseeing the growth of the artist's career; and determining and remedying problems when an artist isn't living up to his potential or his record sales are below expected levels.

9: The Arranger

WHENEVER A SONG is adapted into a commercial recording it has to be "arranged." An arrangement is the creation of musical parts for instruments and vocalists that is a new and different version for the song. The arranger is the person who prepares written parts for various musical instruments and voices that complement and enhance the lyrics and melody to the song and the recording artist's abilities and qualities.

As a songwriter, you should become familiar with the work of the arranger. When (let's think positive!) your songs will be recorded, it will be from the imagination and skill of the arranger that they will be transformed from the simple harmonized melody you have written into a full-blown arrangement. A commercial arrangement is simple in sound yet intricate in the knowledge and extensive in the experience needed to devise it.

When it has been decided that an artist will record a song, the record producer will hire an arranger to write the "charts" or musical arrangements for the planned record. It is common, however, for many individuals to function in the dual capacity of arranger and producer as the skill demanded from each part necessitates talent in the other.

Planning the Arrangement

Before the arranger begins to write the charts he must take certain things into consideration:

1. *The song*. The arranger will first study the song by repeatedly listening to a demonstration recording of it while following along with a lead sheet. (This permits him to see as well as hear what is happening in the song in its simplest form.) After deciding what idea the song is trying to express, the arranger then determines how he can most successfully bring out the best in the music and lyrics. Such factors as harmony, rhythm, and the singer's vocal style (see #2 below) will dictate the particular instrumentation and musical stylings to be used.

2. *The recording artist*. The artist's vocal style, voice quality, and other attributes must be incorporated into the recording. The arranger will try to emphasize the artist's strong points (perhaps range, phrasing, and/or rhythm) and conceal his or her weaknesses. As an example, for a singer weak in singing those notes at the top of his or her vocal range, the arranger can balance the weakness by use of certain techniques such as doubling instruments like strings or reeds in those particular trouble spots.

3. *Market potential*. After studying both the song and the artist's style, the arranger must determine how his arrangements can best capture the market (or markets) the record will be directed at. He will familiarize himself, if he isn't already, with the chart-making songs in the market for which the record is intended to be broadcast and sold in and he will write an arrangement that best frames both song and singer into a commercial and competitive entity for that particular segment of the public.

The Recording Session

After the charts are written, the arranger, producer, and artist will rehearse the songs, examining such variables as the key, tempo, and instrumentation, and make any appropriate changes. The producer will then schedule the recording session. Sometimes, however, a "head" arrangement will be used—that is, a recording session with no prepared charts. The arranger will experiment with various styles of performances (off the top of his head) by the musicians and vocalists who read off a lead sheet. Even with prepared charts, on-the-spot adjustments are often made, when a particular sound doesn't agree with its original conception by any of the principals involved.

Either the arranger or producer will hire a contractor, who in turn will hire the instrumentalists and background vocalists for the session. The contractor's reputation depends on his previous experience in selecting quality musicians and singers. The musicians and background vocalists (except in the case where the performers are members of a group) never see or rehearse their parts before the recording session. The charts usually arrive from the copyist just prior to the session, at which time the musicians and background singers practice any difficult passages and are ready to give a perfect performance at the conductor's cue. It is also the contractor's responsibility to administer the paperwork with regard to tax forms, welfare and pension plans, and other union regulations.

At the recording session, the arranger will conduct the orchestra. Master recordings today often consist of an elaborate instrumentation, including in addition to the usual rhythm, string, and horn sections, instruments previously unused in commercial recordings, such as synthesizers and sound modifiers for woodwind instruments. Once all the parts the arranger has scored are recorded on tape, his job is completed. Payment to the arranger will be a one-time, fixed sum. An arranger does not earn a royalty from sales of a record for which he has written the charts.

The arranger's work, creatively a few notches below the songwriter's, is often the most publicly overlooked contribution to the record. He is the individual who creates the musical environment that pumps life into the record. It is the arranger who musically breathes into the record the flame that sets the song, performer, and listener on fire.

10: Performing Rights Organizations

A PERFORMING RIGHT is the right granted by the United States Copyright Law which, in essence, states that one may not publicly perform for profit * a copyrighted musical work without the copyright owner's permission.

The Origin of Performing Rights Organizations

After the 1909 Copyright Law was sanctioned, performing rights organizations were formed to license copyrighted musical works of their affiliates to anyone who used copyrighted music for profit in public performance. There are three major performing rights organizations now in existence in the United States: the American Society of Composers, Authors and Publishers (ASCAP), formed in 1914 out of the need to insure compliance with the United States Copyright Act of 1909; SESAC Inc., founded in 1931 to license European and American works domestically, on the basis that "music is the common denominator . . . for improved international understanding"; and Broadcast Music, Inc. (BMI), founded in 1940 by a group of broadcasters who wanted to bring about competitive prices in the music licensing market.

---

* Under the copyright law effective January 1, 1978, the public performance does not have to be for profit.

The Role of Performing Rights Organizations

ASCAP and BMI are nonprofit organizations (although BMI is owned by stockholders who receive no dividends or other benefits of ownership) who, along with SESAC, a private organization, collect their license fees from the over seven thousand radio stations, seven hundred television stations, thirty thousand hotels, and numerous other entities such as nightclubs, concert halls, skating rinks, ball parks, steamships, arenas, cabarets, bandstands, cafes, airlines, and wired music services in the United States where music is publicly performed. These outlets, referred to as music users, must obtain licenses from ASCAP, BMI, and/or SESAC to acquire the right to broadcast or have performed on their premises any of the music which is licensed by that particular performing rights organization.

The performing rights organizations (also referred to as clearance agencies) are voluntary associations, and songwriters and music publishers do not have to join. However, it is totally to their advantage to have the performing rights to their songs licensed by one of these organizations so they can collect performance royalties and be protected against infringement. Copyright owners would have a most difficult task, indeed, to act as a clearance agency by monitoring performances and collecting moneys from music users all around the world. Performing rights organizations exist today out of the need to have a central clearinghouse which could replace the burden of direct licensing by copyright owners and to get maximum exposure of copyrighted works.

Determination of Performances

Performing rights organizations determine which of the songs it licenses are being played, how often, and in which media—each organization having its own systems and methods. ASCAP relies on its independent survey of musical performances; BMI uses sampling systems of daily logs furnished to it by the music users, and computerized logging systems; and SESAC relies heavily on chart activity. A more detailed explanation of each organization's methods and systems used to determine performances of its affiliates' songs is set forth in the separate sections describing each organization.

License Fees

The amount of money the music user pays the performing rights organizations is determined by negotiations. License fees to ASCAP and BMI are scaled according to the advertising income for broadcasters and to the size for other music users. License fees to SESAC are based on advertising rates, market areas served, and the size of the music user. For all three organizations, for instance, a fifty-thousand-watt major radio station from a large city will pay more than a five-thousand-watt station from a small town and a large nightclub will pay more than a small coffeehouse. The fees are nondiscriminatory among similarly situated users. After an agreement is reached, the music users receive permission to use the entire repertory of songs from the organization in which they are licensed for a specified period of time.

Distribution

After deducting their operating expenses, ASCAP and BMI distribute all income from license fees to their publisher and writer affiliates by separate checks. Distribution to copyright owners is based upon how often their songs are performed and in which media. Distribution to SESAC affiliates is determined by an allocation committee which makes an objective evaluation of six factors which are set forth in the section on SESAC. Because of the organizations' international affiliations, copyright owners collect performance royalties when their songs are performed in foreign countries.

Publisher and Writer Affiliation

A publishing company may join either ASCAP, BMI, or SESAC and will usually have a subsidiary company affiliated with one of the other organizations. Some publishing companies have two subsidiaries so that they may affiliate with both of the other organizations. Each company will have its own separate legal identity, although there may be one overall conglomerate of which the separate publishing companies are subsidiaries. The reason for multiple affiliations is that a publisher may want to accept a song from a writer who is an affiliate of either ASCAP, BMI, or SESAC. In order for the writer and publisher to receive royalties from his performing rights organization, the song must be written and published by affiliates of that same performing rights organization.

A songwriter may join as a writer affiliate with only one performing rights organization at a time. However, provisions have been made so that writers of different performing rights organizations may collaborate in the writing of songs and collect performance royalties.

Performing rights organizations actively encourage new writers to join because the strength of their catalog will put them in a better negotiating position with users of music. Writers with a strong track record or likelihood to have a song recorded may qualify for the advances that these organizations offer.

Each performing rights organization has a different rate, schedule, and system of payment, so it is important for you to learn everything about the organization before signing their writer's agreement. To find out about these and the benefits offered by each organization, write, phone, or visit your nearest office.

American Society of Composers, Authors and Publishers (ASCAP)

For information on this performing rights organization, contact your nearest ASCAP membership office: 1 Lincoln Plaza, New York, N.Y. 10023; 6430 Sunset Boulevard, Hollywood, Calif. 90028; 2 Music Square West, Nashville, Tenn. 37203. ASCAP licensing offices are located in San Francisco, North Miami, Atlanta, Chicago, New Orleans, Boston, Minneapolis, Cleveland, Detroit, Philadelphia, and Houston.

After the United States Copyright Law was passed in 1909, it was found that many music users, most notably hotel ballrooms, dance halls, and saloons, were making greater profits from customers attracted by public performances of copyrighted musical works without paying for the privilege. This was in direct violation of the 1909 Copyright Law whose purpose was to encourage the creation of new songs by payment to writers whose works were performed commer-

APPLICATION FOR WRITER-MEMBERSHIP
IN THE
American Society of Composers, Authors and Publishers

ONE LINCOLN PLAZA, NEW YORK, N. Y. 10023

The undersigned hereby applies
for membership as a

CHECK   FULL ☐   CHECK   STANDARD ☐   AUTHOR ☐ CHECK

ASSOCIATE ☐   POPULAR PRODUCTION ☐   COMPOSER ☐

in the American Society of Composers, Authors and Publishers, agreeing if and when elected to abide and be bound by the Articles of Association thereof, as now in effect or as may be hereafter amended, and to execute such agreements as may then be in force in identical terms as between the Society and its other members.

The following information is submitted in support of this application:

Please print or type:

Full Name: Mr. Mrs. Miss..

Pseudonyms, if any..

Born at... on .... , 1...........

Citizen of..

Social Security No. ....

The applicant represents that there is in existence or effect no assignment or license, direct or indirect, of non-dramatic performing rights in or to any of the works listed herein, except as such may have been effected with publishers of the said works or by the assignments or licenses of which true copies are hereto annexed.

Musical works of which applicant is composer or author are listed on the reverse side hereof.

Applicant has read the Articles of Association of the American Society of Composers, Authors and Publishers and makes this application with full knowledge of the contents thereof.

Dated at..., 19........

Proposed by ....

Seconded by ....

<table>
<tr><td colspan="2">DO NOT FILL IN THESE SPACES</td></tr>
<tr><td>Rec'd</td><td>, 19.....</td></tr>
<tr><td>Subm't'd.</td><td>, 19.....</td></tr>
<tr><td>Action</td><td></td></tr>
<tr><td>By.</td><td></td></tr>
</table>

Signature of Applicant

Street and Number

City and State

Telephone

(NOTE: An applicant is not required to have his application proposed and seconded. Be sure to keep the Society advised of changes in address and telephone. Also notify Society of all numbers published subsequent to the filing of this application.

(OVER)

LIST OF WORKS

TITLE	YEAR PUBLISHED	AUTHOR	COMPOSER	PUBLISHER

Note: For works based on compositions in the public domain, the title, author and composer of public domain source must be indicated.

cially. The proprietors ignored the law's requirement for them to obtain licenses and thus paid nothing to copyright owners whose works were being publicly performed. To insure compliance with the Copyright Law, a group that included Victor Herbert, John Philip Sousa, and other outstanding composers formed the American Society of Composers, Authors and Publishers in 1914. Although ASCAP was originally founded for this purpose, it has developed into the service organization it functions as today.

ASCAP's only income is from collecting license fees which are distributed to its members "fairly, scientifically, and economically" after its operating expenses are deducted. The most important factor used to determine the distribution of income to its members is the number and kind of performances of a work noted and logged in its survey of performances on radio, television, wired music, and other similar services.

The ASCAP survey separates each music user it licenses into certain categories for which there is a particular method or system used to determine which ASCAP songs are performed and for which a certain amount of performance credits for a played work is given in that category.

Broadcasters, who represent the largest category of music users in the ASCAP survey, are subdivided into 1) television networks, 2) local television stations, and 3) radio stations. The survey treats each of these categories separately:

1. Network television. ASCAP determines which of its works were performed by the program logs and cue sheets that the three U.S. television networks provide.
2. Local television. By sampling *TV Guides,* audiotapes, and cue sheets, ASCAP determines which of its works were performed in this medium.
3. Radio stations. ASCAP makes tapes in units of six hours each of radio station broadcasts around the country. The tapes are sent to New York where performances of ASCAP works are identified. The choice of stations to be sampled is made by computer and includes all classes (size of ASCAP license fees) and regions of radio stations. ASCAP personnel are not aware in advance of which stations are being monitored and when, and neither are the stations being monitored.

Each performance in every category noted and logged in the ASCAP survey of performances is given a certain amount of performance credits, each credit having a monetary value that changes periodically. Writers and publishers receive their royalties based on the amount of money available for distribution and performance credits earned. ASCAP can pay its writers by one of two methods: the "current performance option" which allows members to receive payments as soon as possible and the "four-fund system" which spreads the payments out over a certain period of time and which could possibly relieve tax pressures on substantial earnings by writers. Publishers may receive their royalties only on the "current performance option."

Because ASCAP is a membership association, those songwriters and music publishers who are signatories to its writer and publisher agreements are referred to as "members" rather than "affiliates."

Full writer membership in ASCAP is open to any composer or lyricist of a copyrighted musical work which has been commercially published or recorded. Associate membership is available to writers who have a song copyrighted but which has not been published or recorded. Publisher membership is available to any firm or individual that has one or more songs recorded.

There is no application fee, but annual dues are $10 for full writer members and $50 for publishers.

Broadcast Music, Inc. (BMI)

For information on this performing rights organization, contact your nearest BMI affiliation office: 40 West 57th Street, New York, N.Y. 10019; 6255 Sunset Boulevard, Hollywood, Calif. 90028; 10 Music Square East, Nashville, Tenn. 37203. BMI licensing offices are located in Boston, Coral Gables, Houston, and Chicago.

When BMI was founded in 1940, it offered this statement of policy: "BMI is a completely new force in American music. It is also a means of giving you who make up the musical public an opportunity to hear its music and, most significant of all, an opportunity to grow familiar with the work of composers who previously have not been privileged to put their music before you. BMI has dropped the

BROADCAST MUSIC, INC.

40 West 57th Street   New York, N.Y. 10019

Date

Dear

The following shall constitute the agreement between us:

1. As used in this agreement:

    (a) The word "period" shall mean the term of two years from

to   , and continuing thereafter for additional terms of two years each unless terminated by either party at the end of said initial term or any additional term, upon notice by registered or certified mail not more than six months or less than sixty (60) days prior to the end of any such term.

    (b) The word "works" shall mean:

        (i) All musical and dramatico-musical compositions composed by you alone or with one or more collaborators during the period; and

        (ii) All musical and dramatico-musical compositions composed by you alone or with one or more collaborators prior to the period, except those in which there is an outstanding grant of the right of public performance to a person other than a publisher affiliated with BMI.

2. You agree that:

    (a) Within ten (10) days after the execution of this agreement you will furnish to us two copies of a completed clearance sheet in the form supplied by us with respect to each work heretofore composed by you which has been published in printed copies or recorded commercially or which is being currently performed or which you consider as likely to be performed.

    (b) In each instance that a work for which clearance sheets have not been submitted to us pursuant to sub-paragraph (a) hereof is published in printed copies or recorded commercially or in synchronization with film or tape or is considered by you as likely to be performed. whether such work is composed prior to the execution of this agreement or hereafter during the period, you will promptly furnish to us two copies of a completed clearance sheet in the form supplied by us with respect to each such work.

    (c) If requested by us in writing, you will promptly furnish to us a legible lead sheet or other written or printed copy of a work.

3. The submission of clearance sheets pursuant to paragraph 2 hereof shall constitute a warranty by you that all of the information contained thereon is true and correct and that no performing rights in such work have been granted to or reserved by others except as specifically set forth therein in connection with works heretofore written or co-written by you.

4. You hereby grant to us for the period:

    (a) All the rights that you own or acquire publicly to perform, and to license others to perform, for profit or otherwise, anywhere in the world, any part or all of the works, such rights being granted exclusively to us except to the extent of any prior grants listed on clearance sheets submitted with respect to works heretofore written or co-written by you.

    (b) The non-exclusive right to record, and to license others to record, any part or all of any of the works on electrical transcriptions, wire, tape, film or otherwise, but only for the purpose of performing such work publicly by means of radio and television or for archive or audition purposes and not for sale to the public or for synchronization with motion pictures intended primarily for theatrical exhibition or with programs distributed by means of syndication to broadcasting stations.

(c) The non-exclusive right to adapt, arrange, change and dramatize any part or all of any of the works for performance purposes, and to license others to do so.

5. (a) The rights granted to us by sub-paragraph (a) of paragraph 4 hereof shall not include the right to perform or license the performance of more than one song or aria from an opera, operetta, or musical comedy or more than five minutes from a ballet if such performance is accompanied by the dramatic action, costumes or scenery of that opera, operetta, musical comedy or ballet.

(b) You, together with the publisher and your collaborators, if any, shall have the right jointly, by written notice to us, to exclude from the grant made by sub-paragraph (a) of paragraph 4 hereof performances of more than thirty (30) minutes' duration of a work which is an opera, operetta or musical comedy, but this right shall not apply to a work which is the score of a film originally written for exhibition in motion picture theaters when performed as incorporated in such film, or which is a score originally written for a radio or television program when performed as incorporated in such program.

6. (a) As full consideration for all rights granted to us hereunder, we agree to pay to you, with respect to each of the works in which we obtain and retain exclusive performing rights during the period:

(i) For performances of a work on broadcasting stations in the United States, its territories and possessions and Canada, amounts calculated pursuant to our then current standard practices upon the basis of the then current performance rates generally paid by us to our affiliated writers for similar performances of similar compositions. The number of performances for which you shall be entitled to payment shall be estimated by us in accordance with our then current system of computing the number of such performances.

(ii) All monies received by us from any performing rights licensing organization outside of the United States, its territories and possessions and Canada, which are designated by such performing rights licensing organization as the author's share of foreign performance royalties earned by your works after the deduction of ten percent (10%) of the gross amount thereof to cover our handling charge.

(b) In the case of a work composed by you with one or more collaborators, the sum payable to you hereunder shall be a pro rata share, determined on the basis of the number of collaborators, unless you shall have transmitted to us a copy of an agreement between you and your collaborators providing for a different division of payment.

(c) We shall have no obligation to make payment hereunder with respect to (i) any performance of a work which occurs prior to the date on which we have received from you all of the information and material with respect to such work which is referred to in paragraphs 2 and 3 hereof, or (ii) any performance of a work for which you receive payment of performance royalties from the publisher thereof. You waive the right to receive performance royalties from the publisher of any work with respect to any and all performances thereof for which you receive payment from us hereunder.

7. We will furnish statements to you at least twice during each year of the period showing the number of performances as computed pursuant to sub-paragraph (a) (i) of paragraph 6 hereof and at least once during each year of the period showing the monies due pursuant to sub-paragraph (a) (ii) of paragraph 6 hereof. Each statement shall be accompanied by payment to you, subject to all proper deductions for advances, if any, of the sum thereby shown to be due for such performances.

8. (a) Nothing in this agreement requires us to continue to license the works subsequent to the termination of this agreement. In the event that we continue to license any or all of the works, however, we shall continue to make payments to you for so long as you do not make or purport to make directly or indirectly any grant of performing rights in such works to any other licensing organization. The amounts of such payments shall be calculated pursuant to our then current standard practices upon the basis of the then current performance rates generally paid by us to our affiliated writers for similar performances of similar compositions. You agree to notify us by registered or certified mail of any grant or purported grant by you directly or indirectly of performing rights to any other performing rights organization within ten (10) days from the making of such grant or purported grant and if you fail so to inform us thereof and we make payments to you for any period after the making of any such grant or purported grant, you agree to repay to us all amounts so paid by us promptly on demand. In addition, if we inquire of you by registered or certified mail, addressed to your last known address, whether you have made any such grant or purported grant and you fail to confirm to us by registered or certified mail within thirty (30) days of the mailing of such inquiry that you have not made any such grant or purported grant, we may, from and after such date, discontinue making any payments to you.

(b) Our obligation to continue payment to you after the termination of this agreement for performances outside of the United States, its territories and possessions and Canada shall be dependent upon our receipt in the United States of payments designated by foreign performing rights organizations as the author's share of foreign performance royalties earned by your works. Payment of such foreign royalties shall be subject to deduction of our then current handling charge applicable to our affiliated writers.

(c) In the event that we have reason to believe that you will receive or are receiving payment from a performing rights licensing organization other than BMI for or based on United States and/or Canadian performances of one or more of your works during a period when such works were licensed by us pursuant to this agreement, we shall have the right to withhold payment for such performances from you until receipt of evidence satisfactory to us of the amount so paid to you by such other organization or that you have not been so paid. In the event that you have been so paid, the monies payable by us to you for such performances during such period shall be reduced by the amount of the payment from such other organization. In the event that you do not supply such evidence within eighteen (18) months from the date of our request therefor, we shall be under no obligation to make any payment to you for performances of such works during such period.

9. In the event that you terminate this agreement pursuant to sub-paragraph (a) of paragraph 1 hereof at a time when, after crediting all earnings reflected by the statements rendered to you prior to the effective date of such termination, there remains an unearned balance of advances made to you by us, such termination shall not be effective with respect to the works then embraced by this agreement unless and until thirty (30) days after the unpaid balance of advances shall be repaid by you or until a statement is rendered by us at our normal accounting period showing that such unearned balance of advances has been fully recouped by us.

10. You warrant and represent that you have the right to enter into this agreement; that you are not bound by any prior commitments which conflict with your commitments hereunder; that each of the works, composed by you alone or with one or more collaborators, is original; and that exercise of the rights granted by you herein will not constitute an infringement of copyright or violation of any other right of, or unfair competition with, any person, firm or corporation. You agree to indemnify and hold harmless us and our licensees from and against any and all loss or damage resulting from any claim of whatever nature arising from or in connection with the exercise of any of the rights granted by you in this agreement. Upon notification to us or any of our licensees of a claim with respect to any of the works, we shall have the right to exclude such work from this agreement and/or to withhold payment of all sums which become due pursuant to this agreement or any modification thereof until such claim has been withdrawn, settled or adjudicated.

11. (a) We shall have the right, upon written notice to you, to exclude from this agreement, at any time, any work which in our opinion (i) is similar to a previously existing composition and might constitute a copyright infringement, or (ii) has a title or music or lyric similar to that of a previously existing composition and might lead to a claim of unfair competition, or (iii) is offensive, in bad taste or against public morals, or (iv) is not reasonably suitable for performance.

(b) In the case of works which in our opinion are based on compositions in the public domain, we shall have the right, upon written notice to you, either (i) to exclude any such work from this agreement, or (ii) to classify any such work as entitled to receive only a fraction of the full credit that would otherwise be given for performances thereof.

(c) In the event that any work is excluded from this agreement pursuant to paragraph 10 or sub-paragraph (a) or (b) of this paragraph 11, all rights in such work shall automatically revert to you ten (10) days after the date of our notice to you of such exclusion. In the event that a work is classified for less than full credit under sub-paragraph (b) (ii) of this paragraph 11, you shall have the right, by giving notice to us, within ten (10) days after the date of our letter advising you of the credit allocated to the work, to terminate our rights therein, and all rights in such work shall thereupon revert to you.

12. In each instance that you write, or are employed or commissioned by a motion picture producer to write, during the period, all or part of the score of a motion picture intended primarily for exhibition in theaters, or by the producer of a dramatico-musical work or revue for the legitimate stage to write, during the period, all or part of the musical compositions contained therein, we agree to advise the producer of the film that such part of the score as is written by you may be performed as part of the exhibition of said film in theaters in the United States, its territories and possessions, without compensation to us, or to the producer of the dramatico-musical work or revue that your compositions embodied therein may be performed on the stage with living artists as part of such dramatico-musical work or revue, without compensation to us. In the event that we notify you that we have established a system for the collection of royalties for performance of the scores of motion picture films in theaters in the United States, its territories and possessions, we shall no longer be obligated to take such action with respect to motion picture scores.

13. You make, constitute and appoint us, or our nominee, your true and lawful attorney, irrevocably during the term hereof, in our name or that of our nominee, or in your name, or otherwise, to do all acts, take all proceedings, execute, acknowledge and deliver any and all instruments, papers, documents, process or pleadings that may be necessary, proper or expedient to restrain infringement of and/or to enforce and protect the rights granted by you hereunder, and to recover damages in respect to or for the infringement or other violation of the

said rights, and in our sole judgment to join you and/or others in whose names the copyrights to any of the works may stand; to discontinue, compromise or refer to arbitration, any such actions or proceedings or to make any other disposition of the disputes in relation to the works, provided that any action or proceeding commenced by us pursuant to the provisions of this paragraph shall be at our sole expense and for our sole benefit.

14. You agree that you, your agents, employees or representatives will not, directly or indirectly, solicit or accept payment from writers for composing music for lyrics or writing lyrics to music or for reviewing, publishing, promoting, recording or rendering other services connected with the exploitation of any composition, or permit use of your name or your affiliation with us in connection with any of the foregoing. In the event of a violation of any of the provisions of this paragraph 14, we shall have the right, in our sole discretion, by giving you at least thirty (30) days' notice by registered or certified mail, to terminate this agreement. In the event of such termination no payments shall be due to you pursuant to paragraph 8 hereof.

15. No monies due or to become due to you shall be assignable, whether by way of assignment, sale or power granted to an attorney-in-fact, without our prior written consent. If any assignment of such monies is made by you without such prior written consent, no rights of any kind against us will be acquired by the assignee, purchaser or attorney-in-fact.

16. All disputes of any kind, nature or description whatsoever arising in connection with the terms and conditions of this agreement, or arising out of the performance thereof, or based upon an alleged breach thereof, shall be submitted to arbitration in the City, County and State of New York under the then prevailing rules of the American Arbitration Association by an arbitrator or arbitrators to be selected as follows: Each of us shall by written notice to the other have the right to appoint one arbitrator, provided, however, that if within ten (10) days following the giving of such notice by one of us the other shall not by written notice appoint another arbitrator the first arbitrator appointed shall be the sole arbitrator. If two arbitrators are so appointed, they shall thereupon appoint the third arbitrator, provided that if ten (10) days shall elapse after the appointment of the second arbitrator and the said two arbitrators are unable to agree upon the appointment of the third arbitrator then either of us may, in writing, request the American Arbitration Association to appoint the third arbitrator. The award made in the arbitration shall be binding and conclusive on us and judgment may be, but need not be, entered thereon in any court having jurisdiction. Such award shall include the fixing of the cost of arbitration, which shall be borne by the unsuccessful party.

17. Any notice sent to you pursuant to the terms of this agreement shall be valid if addressed to you at the last address furnished by you in writing to our Department of Writer Administration.

18. This agreement cannot be changed orally and shall be governed and construed pursuant to the laws of the State of New York.

Very truly yours,

BROADCAST MUSIC, INC.

ACCEPTED AND AGREED TO:

By ....

....

bars, and now the new, the young and those you may not have known, can bring you their songs.''

Thus, BMI declared an open door policy to the writers and publishers of the then new forms of music, such as rock 'n' roll and rhythm and blues, who were left unprotected by the performing rights organizations at that time. BMI now has the largest writer and publisher affiliation of any United States performing rights organization.

BMI determines performances of its songs on radio stations by sampling systems. For monitoring BMI songs from the thousands of local radio stations it licenses, BMI uses the following method: Each quarter a certain number of stations provides BMI with a list of the music they use, hour by hour and day by day for one week. The stations are scientifically chosen and represent a cross-section of broadcasting activity and area. From the information the stations provide, song titles, writers, and publishers are identified by computer. Each performance of a BMI work listed is multiplied by a ''factor'' which reflects the ratio of the number of stations logged to the number of stations licensed.

Exactly which stations are being logged at a given time is never known. Even BMI personnel are not aware of which stations are being monitored for a certain time, until that period is over. The sampling is done on a statistical basis and communication with the stations to be logged is done by an independent accounting firm. In this way, stations cannot be influenced in the music they program.

Network television stations provide BMI with daily logs of all music performed. BMI determines which of its works are being performed on local television by a computerized list of all motion pictures and syndicated programs appearing in the approximately 90 issues of *TV Guide* published each week in the United States.

BMI pays its affiliates based on the payment schedule of performances it publishes. This schedule is given to writers and publishers when affiliating. Royalties for a particular song performed on local radio and television represent payment for the number of factored performances during a particular quarter as multiplied by the payment rate for a logged performance of that kind. Payments are made on a quarterly basis.

Writer affiliation is open to the writer of any copyrighted musical work that has been recorded, published, or is ''likely to be performed.'' Publishers may join when they have a recorded or "likely to be recorded" song. There is no application fee or annual dues for writers, but there is a $25 application fee for publishers, who pay no annual dues.

SESAC Inc.

For information on this performing rights and mechanical rights organization, contact your nearest SESAC office: 10 Columbus Circle, New York, New York 10019; 11 Music Circle South, Nashville, Tenn. 37203.

SESAC (formerly called "The Society of European Stage Authors and Composers") was founded by Paul Heinecke, in 1931, on the principle that "Music is the common denominator . . . a communications instrument barrier international in scope that knows no language barrier. Man's creative melodies provide the ideal setting for improved international understanding."

At its inception, the SESAC catalog consisted of works published primarily by European firms. With the advent of broadcasting, its catalog grew to include works primarily from gospel and country and western music publishers. It now enjoys, however, the full span of musical diversity.

Until 1972, SESAC was primarily a publisher-oriented organization. At that time they wished to sign up writers directly and established a "writer's program." Their roster now includes new and established songwriters representative of all areas of music.

Of the three licensing organizations, SESAC is the only one to represent the publisher in three separate areas: performance rights, mechanical rights, and synchronization rights. They maintain extensive mechanical licensing, copyright clearance, and index departments where records are kept of all licenses issued and of the complete histories of the works in their catalog.

The amount of money writers and publishers earn as SESAC affiliates is determined by an allocation committee which is composed of officers of the organization. Distribution to publishers and writers is based on the following six factors: total number of copyrights; their diversity; growth of the catalog (new copyrights); seniority; overall promotional activity; and, of course, the most important, performances. Under the performances category, SESAC relies heavily on the chart activity of its affiliates' songs. SESAC also pays minimum release money of $150 each to the writer and publisher for every song which appears on a bona fide record label with national distribution. Additional payments are made for trade picks and cover recordings.

SESAC grants three bonuses for songs which have remained on the charts for a certain time period and have achieved "crossover" activity:

1. A 25 percent longevity bonus for those compositions which have been on all three charts for a minimum of 15 weeks
2. A 25 percent bonus for those songs which cross over from one chart to another
3. A 10 percent carryover bonus for songs which have either attained a top ten average chart position or have been on the charts for 15 weeks or more.

The money paid to writer and publisher affiliates based on chart activity and bonuses can earn the writer and publisher $30,000 each, as the following example illustrates (subject to periodic change):

#1 ON POP CHART	$35,000
25% Longevity Bonus (15 wks. on charts) $35,000 × 25% =	8,750
Crossover Bonus #1 ON COUNTRY CHART = $25,000 $25,000 × 25% =	6,250
Carryover Bonus (Top Ten activity OR 15 wk. longevity) $50,000 × 10% = $5,000 (× 2 years) =	10,000
Total Chart and Bonus Earnings	$60,000

SESAC – PUBLISHER

Affiliation Agreement

AGREEMENT made this...day of.., 19   , in New York, N. Y.,

between ....

.... of ....

(hereinafter called PUBLISHER) and SESAC, Inc., Coliseum Tower, 10 Columbus Circle, New York 19, N. Y. (hereinafter called SESAC).

WITNESSETH

In consideration of One Dollar and other good and valuable considerations by each of the parties to the other in hand paid, the receipt of which is hereby acknowledged and of the mutual promises of the parties herein contained, it is agreed between them as follows:

1. The word PUBLICATIONS as herein used shall include the titles, texts, librettos, words and music of all literary works, musical works, compositions, musical compositions, books and other works with music, collections, folios, dramatico-musical works, individual selections, fragments and arrangements from dramatico-musical works, and all arrangements, adaptations, versions, editions and translations of any or all of the foregoing works, whether published or unpublished, printed or in manuscript or any other form, mechanical or otherwise and whether or not copyright has been secured in same, in which the PUBLISHER now and hereafter during the term of this agreement, directly and indirectly, has any right, title or interest or control whatsoever in whole or in part, and which the PUBLISHER creates, writes, composes, acquires, owns, controls, issues, prints or publishes or causes to be printed or published under PUBLISHER'S or any other name.

2. The PUBLISHER hereby sells, assigns, transfers, grants, sets over and delivers unto SESAC, for the world, and for the full term of this contract and all extensions and renewals thereof, all rights of every kind and nature existing or which may hereafter come into existence, in all PUBLICATIONS now owned or controlled, and which may be owned or controlled by the PUBLISHER during the term of this contract, and all extensions or renewals thereof, and existing under all domestic and foreign copyrights of such PUBLICATIONS, including by way of specification but not limitation, the sole rights to publicly perform, exhibit, present, represent, produce and reproduce; to record, transcribe and otherwise mechanically record or reproduce by any method, whether now or hereafter used or known, and to license, vend or otherwise dispose of pressings, reproductions or copies thereof; to synchronize and otherwise use with sound motion pictures; together with all rights in said PUBLICATIONS for radio, broadcasting, facsimile, television, motion pictures, sound motion pictures, theatres and other places of entertainment; and together with the right to arrange, adapt, dramatize, translate and make any changes, and additions of new matter in the titles, texts, librettos, words and music of any PUBLICATIONS in order to exploit, license or otherwise use any of said PUBLICATIONS; except only that the PUBLISHER retains all publishing rights consisting of the right to publish, print, vend and distribute copies of the PUBLICATIONS. Nothing contained in this agreement shall be construed as impairing any of the rights and obligations of the parties hereto under any separate Royalty Agreement between them providing for certain royalty payments by SESAC to PUBLISHER.

3. SESAC is hereby authorized and empowered to enter into and to grant, in its own name or in the name of the PUBLISHER, any exclusive and/or non-exclusive contracts and licenses authorizing the use of any or all of the PUBLICATIONS, to the extent of any or any of SESAC'S rights therein,

    (a) in separate individual transactions involving all or any of the PUBLISHER'S PUBLICATIONS, wherein separate payment is made by the licensee for use of one or more of the PUBLICATIONS, and not for use on a collective basis as defined in subdivision (b) of this paragraph. In the case of such separate individual transactions, SESAC is hereby authorized and empowered to grant and enter into such contracts and licenses as herein provided for the full term or any part thereof of any domestic and foreign copyrights existing or any renewals thereof in respect of any of the PUBLICATIONS.

    (b) in collective transactions involving all or any of the PUBLISHER'S PUBLICATIONS with all or any of the publications of any other publisher or publishers. With respect to licenses based on such collective transactions granted by SESAC for a period in excess of the term of this contract, PUBLISHER'S PUBLICATIONS shall continue to be included in such collective licenses during such excess period. During such excess period, said PUBLICATIONS shall be included in such licenses on a non-exclusive basis only.

It is agreed that SESAC shall have the sole right to determine, fix and regulate all of the terms, conditions and fees for all licenses and contracts affecting all or any of said PUBLICATIONS under 3 (a) and 3 (b) hereof, and it shall also have the right in its judgment and discretion to authorize the use of PUBLICATIONS gratuitously.

The PUBLISHER hereby ratifies and confirms all contracts and licenses which may be made by SESAC pursuant to the authority hereof or which have been heretofore made by SESAC under which use shall be made of PUBLISHER'S PUBLICATIONS, and hereby irrevocably constitutes and appoints SESAC or its nominee as its true and lawful attorney, in its name or in the name of the PUBLISHER, to make, sign, execute, acknowledge and deliver any and all contracts and licenses pursuant to the authority of this paragraph.

4. SESAC agrees that during the term hereof, it will in good faith use its best efforts to enter into contracts and licenses with broadcasting stations, wherein SESAC shall grant to such stations the right to publicly perform said PUBLICATIONS and the publications of other publishers and agrees to make payments to the PUBLISHER and other publishers in the amounts to be determined as hereinafter provided.

5. It is agreed that from all sums collected in respect of contracts and licenses entered into by SESAC pursuant to paragraph 3 hereof, SESAC shall deduct all expenses incurred (a) in efforts to negotiate or procure contracts, licenses, compromises, settlements or in the prosecution and defense of claims of any kind, including infringements, or in any other legal proceedings affecting the subject matter of this contract; (b) in securing protection in copyright and other matters; (c) by way of license or other fees or special taxes of any kind imposed by any municipal, state or federal laws or regulations as a condition of carrying on any of SESAC'S business activities; (d) in protecting SESAC, or its licensees, or its affiliated publishers (if such action be deemed proper in the sole discretion of SESAC) from any consequences resulting from rules or regulations of any governmental agency or authority, from statutes, whether municipal, state, federal or foreign, from activities of trade or labor organizations, from industry conditions, or from other causes beyond the control of SESAC; (e) in obtaining and issuing promotional material and advertising, or in providing equipment and supplies in connection therewith; (f) in public relations and in general administration and other services incidental to any of the purposes aforesaid; (g) in any other services including those of attorneys and other representatives engaged in connection with any of the foregoing activities; (h) in traveling in connection with any of the foregoing purposes; and (i) in any other manner deemed necessary by SESAC in the exploitation and administration of any rights vested in SESAC.

6. (a) The expenses incurred in connection with separate individual transactions involving exclusively all or any of the PUBLISHER'S PUBLICATIONS shall be deducted pursuant to paragraph 5 hereof from the revenues received from said separate individual transactions for licenses granted by SESAC for the use of rights in PUBLICATIONS, and after making such deductions, fifty per cent (50%) of the net gains and profits remaining from said separate individual transactions shall be retained by SESAC, and the other fifty per cent (50%) shall be paid by SESAC to the PUBLISHER, or said expenses referred to in this sub-paragraph 6 (a) may in SESAC'S sole discretion be deducted from the revenues received from collective transactions as an expense deduction under paragraph 6 (b) hereof.

    (b) The expenses incurred in connection with collective licenses or transactions involving the publications of more than one of SESAC'S affiliated publishers shall be deducted pursuant to paragraph 5 hereof from the revenues received from collective licenses or transactions, for licenses granted by SESAC for the use of rights in PUBLICATIONS, and after making such deductions, fifty per cent (50%) of the net gains and profits remaining from revenues received from collective licenses or transactions shall be retained by SESAC, and the other fifty per cent (50%) shall be allocated and distributed quarter annually by SESAC, on a basis, method, system, quota and formula and to such extent as shall be determined by SESAC from time to time, and which shall, in the reasonable judgment and discretion of SESAC, result in an equitable allocation and distribution among SESAC'S affiliated publishers.

7. SESAC agrees to remit to PUBLISHER its net fifty per cent (50%) share under paragraph 6 (a), and its allocated share under paragraph 6 (b) in quarterly distributions to be made within ninety (90) days following the end of each calendar quarter.

8. Nothing herein contained shall be construed as entitling PUBLISHER to participate (a) in revenues derived from the manufacture, sale, rental or distribution by SESAC of transcriptions, recordings, films or other types of mechanical reproductions, printed material, or any other tangible media or form of merchandise, nor (b) in revenues derived by SESAC from any kind of business activities except from the direct licensing of public performances of PUBLICATIONS and from the direct licensing of mechanical rights in PUBLICATIONS for use in transcriptions, recordings, films or other types of mechanical reproductions manufactured, sold, rented or distributed by others than SESAC or its authorized agents.

9. The PUBLISHER agrees that it will immediately send and refer to SESAC all correspondence and inquiries received by it relating to any of the rights herein assigned and shall notify all such inquirers to communicate with SESAC directly.

10. The PUBLISHER represents and warrants that it owns and controls and will own and control all rights now and hereafter assigned under this agreement and there are no outstanding prior assignments or contracts for the use of any of said rights which would affect the grant to SESAC hereunder; that it has the full right and power to make this contract and more particularly that it has the full right and power to make the assignment hereinbefore set forth; that all of the PUBLICATIONS are and will be original compositions and/or arrangements of original compositions or of public domain works or reprints thereof, and that none of them will infringe upon any other copyrighted work; that all rights herein assigned to SESAC hereunder are the sole and exclusive property of the PUBLISHER; that the PUBLISHER has obtained, and will obtain, in respect of all PUBLICATIONS, written agreements signed by all of the authors and composers of said PUBLICATIONS granting to the PUBLISHER all of the rights assigned to SESAC hereunder; that all of the rights now and hereafter assigned to SESAC hereunder are and will be free and clear from any liens, claims or demands of any kind, and that there exists and will exist no adverse claims of any kind in respect of any rights acquired by SESAC hereunder; and that no foreign or domestic performing rights licensing society, organization, or any other person, firm, corporation or association has any rights in or claims to any of the rights assigned to SESAC herein.

The PUBLISHER agrees to defend, indemnify, and save and hold SESAC, its agents, servants, officers and employees, and its subsidiaries, assignees, nominees, licensees, the advertisers of its licensees, and their respective agents, servants, officers and employees, free and harmless of and from any and all claims, demands, suits, judgments, and recoveries, including attorney's fees, which may be made or brought against them, or any of them, arising out of the grant of any of the rights herein, or arising out of any kind of use herein provided for of any or all of said PUBLICATIONS. This indemnity agreement shall apply to any claim, demand, suit, judgment or recovery which shall at any time be made either during or after the term of this contract or any renewal thereof.

11. The PUBLISHER agrees to secure, and to execute and deliver to SESAC, upon its request, and in such form as may be requested by it, such additional documents, instruments, agreements and assignments as SESAC may request and agrees to make and do such other acts or things as may be necessary or may be requested by SESAC, to carry out more effectually the purposes of this agreement, and the PUBLISHER does hereby irrevocably constitute and appoint SESAC or its nominee its true and lawful attorney, in its name or in the name of the PUBLISHER, to make, sign, execute, acknowledge and deliver, to SESAC or to others, all documents, instruments, agreements and assignments requested by it hereunder.

12. The PUBLISHER agrees to secure and maintain domestic and international copyright registration and protection and copyright renewals, covering all PUBLICATIONS.

13. The PUBLISHER agrees to deliver to SESAC upon the signing of this contract a list of all PUBLICATIONS, which list shall set forth (a) the titles of all printed and unprinted PUBLICATIONS, (b) the names of all authors and composers of such PUBLICATIONS, (c) the copyright registration numbers of all PUBLICATIONS, with dates of publications, (d) the titles of all PUBLICATIONS which have been mechanically recorded, including the names of the manufacturers, the catalog numbers, and the names of the recording artists; and the PUBLISHER undertakes and agrees to furnish to SESAC, promptly, and from time to time, like data in respect of all PUBLICATIONS hereafter existing during the term of this contract and all renewals and extensions thereof. The PUBLISHER agrees to furnish promptly to SESAC, not less than three (3) copies of each PUBLICATION heretofore printed and which may be hereafter printed, and two (2) pressings of each phonograph record on which any of the PUBLICATIONS have been or shall be recorded.

14. SESAC shall have the right to exclude from the terms and operation of this contract, at any time, any of the PUBLICATIONS, which, in its sole opinion, are similar to any other existing work, or which might constitute an infringement of any other existing work, or in respect of which any dispute or adverse claim may exist, or which might constitute unfair competition as regards any other existing work, or the title, words or music of any other existing work, or which is offensive, immoral, or in bad taste, or which is not suitable for performance, recording or any other use. SESAC shall also have the right to restrict the performance or other use of any of the PUBLICATIONS.

15. This contract and the grant herein shall be for a term of ten (10) years from .... 19...... (and in respect of all contracts and licenses granted by SESAC pursuant to paragraph 3 (a) hereof, shall be for the full terms of all such contracts and licenses, which contracts and licenses so granted pursuant to paragraph 3 (a) shall survive the cancellation or termination of this contract under this paragraph or paragraph 16 during the original or any extended or renewal term hereof) and shall continue for successive terms of ten (10) years each upon all of the same terms and provisions of this contract.

Either party shall have the right and privilege to cancel this contract or any successive extension or renewal thereof upon three (3) months prior written notice, to the other party by United States registered mail return receipt requested, such cancellation notice to be effective at the end of the original period or renewal period during which it may be given; the cancellation or termination of this contract under this paragraph or paragraph 16 shall not affect the unexpired term of any contract or license granted by SESAC pursuant to paragraph 3 (b) hereof.

16. SESAC may terminate this contract at any time upon thirty (30) days prior written notice by United States registered mail in the event that: (a) the PUBLISHER shall make an assignment for the benefit of creditors, or a voluntary or involuntary petition in bankruptcy shall be filed by or against the PUBLISHER, or (b) the PUBLISHER shall not, during any contract year of this agreement, print, publish and place on sale saleable copies of at least fifty (50) copyrighted musical compositions not previously copyrighted and published, or (c) if the PUBLISHER shall, at any time during the term hereof, engage in the business of writing, composing, arranging, printing, or publishing lyrics or music for amateur or professional writers or composers, and charging or exacting a fee or other payment therefor, it being agreed by the parties hereto that such business practices are not generally favored by publishers in the music publishing business or by the music industry, (d) if the PUBLISHER shall fail to comply with the provisions of paragraph 13 of this agreement, or (e) there shall be a change in the management or control of the PUBLISHER.

The failure of SESAC to exercise its right of termination under this paragraph at any given time shall not be deemed a waiver of SESAC'S rights to subsequently terminate by virtue of any prior breach or any subsequent breach.

17. No further payments shall be due or payable to the PUBLISHER subsequent to the date on which termination of this contract becomes effective pursuant to paragraph 15 or 16, except in respect of any licenses and contracts granted or entered into by SESAC pursuant to the authority of paragraph 3 (a) hereof from which revenues are actually received by SESAC.

18. The PUBLISHER hereby irrevocably constitutes and appoints SESAC or its nominee its true and lawful attorney, in the name of the PUBLISHER or in its own name, to do all acts and things, take all proceedings, and make, sign, execute, acknowledge and deliver any and all instruments, papers, documents, process or pleadings which may be necessary, desirable or proper to restrain infringements, or to enforce and protect any of the rights acquired by it hereunder, or to recover damages in respect of the infringement or violation of any such rights, or to settle, compromise and give a release in respect of any infringement or violation of any such rights upon terms and conditions to be determined by SESAC in its sole discretion and SESAC may in its sole judgment, join the PUBLISHER, and anyone else, in any action, proceeding, disposition or settlement whatsoever, under this paragraph. SESAC shall not be obligated to institute any action or proceeding for the enforcement of any of the rights mentioned in this agreement. Any settlements resulting in recoveries or payments received by SESAC under this paragraph, after deducting expenses in accordance with paragraph 5 herein, shall be accounted for by SESAC in accordance with paragraph 6 of this agreement.

19. This agreement, and the provisions hereof, shall be binding upon and inure to the benefit of the respective parties hereto, their legal representatives, successors and assigns, provided, however, that the assignment by the PUBLISHER of this contract or any interest therein, or of any monies due or to become due, by reason of the terms hereof, without the written consent of SESAC shall be void.

20. It is further agreed that this contract shall be construed in accordance with the laws of the State of New York and with applicable Federal laws.

21. This agreement may not be changed, modified or discharged orally.

IN WITNESS WHEREOF, the parties hereto have caused this contract to be signed, executed and sealed the day and year first above written.

....
PUBLISHER

By .... L. S.

SESAC, Inc.

By ....

Form: PR 104 ☆☆

This figure does not include money earned for single releases, album cuts, trade picks, cover records, television performances, etc.

Publisher affiliation is open to any company actively involved in the music business whose compositions are distributed commercially, used in recordings, and performed by the broadcasting industry. Writer membership is open to those whose music is suitable for commercial recording. There is no fee for publisher or writer affiliation with SESAC.

11: Mechanical Rights Organizations

A MECHANICAL RIGHT is the right of a copyright owner to profit from the mechanical reproduction of his songs. Mechanical reproduction of a song includes use of the copyright in records, tapes (reel-to-reel, eight-track, and cassette), electrical transcriptions and audio tapes for broadcast and background music purposes. The money collected from use of the copyright with regard to these sources is called mechanical royalties. Similar to the agencies which collect performance royalties are those referred to as mechanical rights organizations.

The Compulsory License

The law provides for every copyright owner to permit the recording of his song by other parties once that song has been initially recorded with that owner's permission. This provision is referred to as the compulsory license and its purpose is to prevent the monopoly proprietors would have in authorizing recordings of their copyrights. Under this provision, the person seeking such license must serve a notice of his intention to use the compulsory license and pay the copyright owner the statutory royalty for each phonorecord manufactured.* The compulsory license provision is implemented under

---

* Distributed, rather than manufactured, after January 1, 1978.

the 1909 Copyright Law by a requirement that the copyright proprietor must file Form U, "Notice of Use," with the Copyright Office when he uses the composition for mechanical reproduction himself or authorizes others to do so. Filing of "Notice of Use" will no longer be required after December 31, 1977.

Effective January 1, 1978, the person or company who wants the compulsory license must serve a notice of intention on the copyright owner within 30 days after making and before distributing any phonorecords of the work or file a notice of his intention with the Copyright Office if its registration or public records do not identify the copyright owner by name and address. To be entitled to receive royalties under a compulsory license, the copyright owner must be identified in the registration or other public records of the Copyright Office.

Negotiated Licenses

What often happens in the music industry is that record companies will negotiate with a copyright owner to vary the "compulsory licensing" provisions of the law; specifically, to pay a royalty lower than the statutory rate, to account for records manufactured and sold, rather than manufactured, and to account on a quarterly rather than a monthly basis.

Another condition in which negotiated licenses may be used is with respect to the first recording of a copyrighted song. The condition of compulsory license does not apply here. The copyright owner is free to select and impose his own terms for permission to use his composition. The owner may, therefore, require a higher mechanical royalty or insist on future recordings of his other copyrights by the artist at hand, although this does not often happen.

Mechanical Royalty Rate

Effective January 1, 1978, the statutory royalty with respect to compulsory licensing for recordings of music will be two and three-quarter cents (raised from two cents) or one-half cent per minute of playing time, whichever amount is larger. This royalty is divided equally between writer and publisher, except in cases where an American lyric is written to a foreign song, in which case the lyricist would earn a smaller percentage, determined by negotiations with the American publisher.

The Role of Mechanical Rights Organizations

Mechanical rights organizations license record and tape companies on behalf of their affiliated copyright owners to use their copyrights. The mechanical rights organizations collect all royalties earned by their affiliates and after deducting their service charge pay the balance of such earnings to these publishers. The publishers in turn pay the songwriter his share of this income. Mechanical rights organizations also regularly audit record companies' books to make sure publishers are paid fairly.

Mechanical rights organizations also collect synchronization fees if requested by their publisher members. The synchronization fee is for use of the song (copyright) in timed-relation to the motion picture or videotape. These fees are generally arrived at by negotiations between the film producer and the mechanical rights organization acting on behalf of the publisher member. The synchronization fee covers a wide area such as theatrical motion pictures, nontheatrical motion pictures, public and pay television.

Mechanical rights organizations are actively involved, along with record companies and music publishers, in finding and prosecuting individuals who engage in the illegal duplication of records and tapes.

Mechanical Rights Organizations

The Harry Fox Agency, Inc. (110 East 59th Street, New York, New York 10022) is the oldest and largest of all the mechanical rights organizations in the United States. It was formed by a group of music publishers to administer their mechanical licenses and has now grown as a collection agency of mechanical rights royalties for approximately three-quarters of all American music publishers. The agency charges a small percentage of the mechanical royalties music publishers earn for their collection services. Their authorized percentage is 5 percent of gross receipts from publishers whose annual income is less than $25,000 and 3¼ percent of gross receipts for publishers whose annual income is greater than this sum. They reserve the right as economic conditions dictate to lower their fees.

The Harry Fox Agency acts in other capacities. They represent publishers for the use of their compositions in motion picture synchronization, television films, and videotapes. They also make sure their publisher affiliates are paid fairly by regularly conducting audits of all record manufacturers they collect royalties from.

SESAC Inc. (10 Columbus Circle, New York, New York 10022) handles all negotiations with record companies, producers of syndicated programs, and any other firm that engages in the mechanical reproduction of the copyrighted works on behalf of its publisher affiliates. SESAC also negotiates synchronization licenses for use of copyrights owned by its affiliates in motion pictures. SESAC's charges for administering mechanical reproduction and synchronization licenses range from a low of 3½ percent to a high of 10 percent for synchronization licenses.

The American Mechanical Rights Association (AMRA) (250 West 57th Street, New York, New York 10019) collects all mechanical reproduction royalties for both the songwriter and music publisher and can pay each separately on a quarterly basis. AMRA licenses record companies in the United States and Canada on behalf of its music writer and music publisher members and automatically collects mechanical royalties on their behalf when records containing their copyrights are released throughout the world.

Copyright Service Bureau Ltd. (CSB) (221 West 57th Street, New York, New York 10019) began in 1965 when a group of music publishers asked Walter Hofer, its founder, for assistance in collecting their royalties. In addition to collecting mechanical royalties the Copyright Service Bureau is now an administrative organization that provides many services: handles songwriting royalty statements, files all copyright registrations, prepares all domestic and foreign contracts, files and updates information with the appropriate performing rights organizations, and can, at the publisher's request, arrange for all printing of sheet music, folios, and songbooks and collect all royalties earned by these sources.

For songwriters who can obtain recordings of their songs and wish to self-publish their copyrights, the CSB can perform the necessary copyright and financial administrations. The CSB's charge for services is scaled according to the income and types of services used by its affiliates. CSB has offices in England, France, Germany, and Japan that make thorough checks of the royalties accounted for by the foreign rights societies in those countries.

Mietus Copyright Management (MCM) (527 Madison Avenue, New York, New York 10022) handles the full administration relating to a music publisher's business. Services performed are copyrighting, clearance of compositions with the performing rights organization, making certain that all proper writer and publisher agreements exist, collection of all mechanical income, seeing to it that foreign income is realized by basically utilizing the governmental mechanical agencies in all foreign countries, and attending to all other business functions which are normally that of a music publisher. MCM charges a publisher 10 percent of gross income received with an initial agreement requiring minimum quarterly fees determined by the size of the catalog being administered.

12: Other Organizations of Importance to the Songwriter

THE AMERICAN GUILD *of Authors and Composers* (*AGAC*) (40 West 57th Street, New York, N.Y. 10019 and 6430 Sunset Boulevard, Hollywood, California 90028) was founded in 1931 by three prominent songwriters—Edgar Leslie, Billy Rose, and George Meyer —as a result of their desire for a standard contract for songwriters. Originally named the Songwriters' Protective Association (SPA), the name was changed to its current one in 1958. It is a voluntary songwriters' protective association run by and for songwriters. It represents and defends songwriters in their dealings with music publishers.

Membership in AGAC offers the songwriter several benefits, including the provision of an AGAC contract for use with music publishers, a royalty collection service, a collaboration service, a copyright renewal service, and an estates administration service for a small annual percentage of his royalties. For writers who want to be their own publishers, AGAC also provides financial administration of their catalog.

The Composers and Lyricists Guild of America (*CLGA*) (6565 Sunset Boulevard, Hollywood, California 90028) is a labor union which represents composers and lyricists who write for motion pictures and television. The CLGA acts on behalf of its members for contract negotiations with producers and film production companies.

Membership is open to writers who have had one assignment in this medium—writing such things as movie or television themes, film scores, or background music.

The Country Music Association, Inc. (*CMA*) (7 Music Circle North, Nashville, Tennessee 37203) is a professional association whose purpose is to promote country music in its entirety. It has been instrumental in increasing the number of radio stations nationwide playing country music; in increasing country music performances on television and live shows; in increasing sales of country music records, and in gaining larger acceptance for country music throughout the world. Membership is open to writers who derive a portion of their income from country music.

The Nashville Songwriters Association, International (*NSAI*) (25 Music Square West, Nashville, Tennessee 37203) was formed in 1967 and is a nonprofit organization whose purpose is to advance the profession of songwriting. Membership in the NSAI is available to all songwriters.

The Gospel Music Association (*GMA*) (38 Music Square West, Nashville, Tennessee 37203) was formed in 1964 to promote the growth of gospel music in its entirety. The GMA annually presents its ''Dove'' awards for recognition in such categories as Gospel Song of the Year, Gospel Songwriter of the Year, and Best Male and Female Vocalists of the Year. The GMA also publishes an annual directory and yearbook which contains lists of record and publishing companies with names and addresses and information on how to reach various gospel artists.

Membership in the GMA is available in two categories: trade level membership—which requires applicants to be earning a percentage of their income by writing, publishing, recording, or performing gospel music, or be employed in a company involved with gospel music; and associate membership—open to anyone who is interested in and supports gospel music.

The National Academy of Recording Arts and Sciences (*NARAS*) (4444 Riverside Drive, Suite 202, Burbank, California 91505), established in 1957, is an organization dedicated to the advancement of sound recordings. NARAS represents all individuals who contribute creatively to the making of a record. These are songwriters, producers, arrangers, conductors, singers, musicians, actors, engineers, album designers, art directors, liner note writers, and photographers. Active NARAS members are eligible to vote for the Grammy Awards which this organization annually presents.

NARAS has chapters in New York, Chicago, Atlanta, Memphis, Nashville, and San Francisco where periodic membership meetings are held that include discussions about songwriting and copyright law.

To become a member, a songwriter must have written six songs that were recorded and commercially released or one selection which has been recorded and commercially released by not less than six recording artists. Active (voting) membership is available for songwriters and publishers may join as associate (nonvoting) members.

The American Composers Alliance (ACA) (170 West 74th Street, New York, New York 10023) is an organization comprised of members who compose serious concert music. Established in 1938, the ACA helps to further the syllabus of serious music and its members' careers. They take the unpublished works of their members and make them available to music schools, libraries, music dealers, and performers. The ACA can act on behalf of its composer/members as publishers and negotiate such licenses for mechanical and synchronization rights.

13: Songwriter Contracts

IF A PUBLISHER accepts your song and offers you a contract, protect yourself from any unfair contract terms by understanding some basic provisions a songwriter should be entitled to. Contracts vary from publisher to publisher and the eager, unknowing songwriter might hastily sign a contract unfavorable for him.

Investigate the Publisher Before Signing

Before you sign a contract with a publisher, you should try to learn as much about him as possible. Somes questions the writer should seek answers to are: Does the publisher actively go out and obtain recordings? Has he published any hits? What kind of catalog does he have? What kind of reputation does he have? Is he involved in any lawsuits? Whom else has he published? Signing with a publisher who is unable or unwilling to exploit your song is worse than not signing at all.

Recommended Contract Terms

The following are some important conditions recommended to be included in your songwriter's contract. The terms are negotiable and you or your attorney should attempt to have as many as possible, if not all, included in your contract.

Reversion of ownership for nonpublication. If the publisher fails to get you a commercial record release within a set period of time, usually one year, he must either reassign the copyright to you or pay you a sum of money you both agree upon to retain the publishing rights to the song for another specified period of time.

Reversion of ownership for reassignment without consent. If the publisher decides to assign your copyright to another publisher without your permission, then you are entitled to reclaim ownership to the song, if you wish. If, however, he sells his entire catalog, the new proprietor retains ownership.

Reversion of ownership for noninspection. If the publisher does not permit you to an audit regarding your song, copyright ownership reverts to you. You or your certified public accountant should always have the right to audit and inspect the publisher's and his licensee's books throughout the contract period as long as reasonable notice is given to the publisher and the inspection occurs during normal business hours.

Content changes. The publisher cannot make any changes in your song (i.e. title, lyric, or music) without your permission.

Copyright renewal. For contracts signed prior to January 1, 1978, your agreement should state that upon expiration of the original term of copyright all publishing rights revert to you. You are then free to renegotiate terms with him, publish it yourself, or assign the rights to another publisher. Contracts signed from January 1, 1978, and on will make no mention of a renewal period as there is only one copyright term under the new law.

Demo charges. All demo costs should be paid by the publisher. Some publishers attempt to charge the songwriter 50 percent of these costs with the charges to be deducted against future royalties of that song, but you should avoid this. Demo charges should be the sole responsibility of the publisher.

Time limit for payment. The contract should specify the number of times each year that the publisher will pay the writer royalties (the royalty period) and in addition should require payment within a specified time period after the close of each royalty payment period.

No time limit for objection. A time limit will often be placed in a contract during which the songwriter can object to a royalty statement. Attempt to have a clause included stating there is "no time limit for objection" against any royalty statements you receive.

Advances. Any advance you are given must be deducted only against the song for which you were given it and not to any other songs he publishes of yours.

Percentage of royalties. The songwriter shall receive 50 percent of the gross receipts the publisher receives of domestic royalties on mechanical reproductions, electrical transcriptions, and synchronization licenses. (The songwriter and publisher each receive performance royalties by separate checks from their performing rights organization.) For sheet music sales, attempt to receive 10 percent of the retail selling price per copy of sheet music sold.

Percentage of royalties for unspecified uses. For all income the song earns from unspecified royalty percentages or unspecified sources in the contract, the contract should call for the writer to receive 50 percent of this. This should include all income obtained from compulsory license fees from jukeboxes, educational, and cable television systems commencing January 1, 1978.

Songwriter credit. The writer's name must be present on any license or publication of the song the publisher makes.

Publisher advances. For any advance the publisher receives, such as for foreign publication, the songwriter shall receive 50 percent of this money.

Foreign royalty percentage. The songwriter should receive 50 percent of all moneys received from foreign sources computed on the publisher's net receipts.

Exclusive Songwriter Contracts

At some point in your career you might be asked by a publisher to sign an "exclusive songwriter's agreement." For singer-songwriters, this might come from the publishing arm of a record company or producer. Since these contracts provide for long-term relationships, the songwriter must be particularly careful that his contract is fair and is in his best interests.

The standard "exclusive songwriter's agreement" calls for an initial term of contract between songwriter and publisher for a period of fifty-two weeks, with the option of one-year renewals by the publisher. The songwriter should, therefore, insist on having as many as possible of the aforementioned conditions included in his contract, particularly the provision that the publisher must obtain a commercial recording of his song within a specified time period or else reassign the copyright to the writer. In cases where the writer also renders his services as artist, he should obtain a clause in his contract stating he shall be recorded and have the record released within a year of signing, otherwise the contract becomes void.

Songwriters should also avoid granting the publisher the rights to any and all previously written songs. It is possible you signed agreements with other publishers for songs you previously wrote and the new publisher is not entitled to those rights.

A term usually included in "exclusive songwriter's agreements" is the right of the publisher to assign or sell this agreement to a third party. Songwriters should attempt to place limitations upon this clause as an incapable new publisher could jeopardize the songwriter's career.

Songwriters under exclusive contract agreements should receive payment for their services either in the form of an advance or by weekly or monthly salary. Writers signed to record companies as performers as well should be aware that their artist contracts will provide that recording costs for their sessions will be deducted by the record company against future royalties of those particular recordings owed to them as artists.

The AGAC Songwriter's Contract

The American Guild of Authors and Composers (AGAC) has a substantial and growing number of music publishers who are signatories to the AGAC contract. It provides for songwriters all the benefits and protection to which they are entitled. According to AGAC and many music industry personnel, songwriters "get the best writers' contract available" with the AGAC songwriter's agreement.

AMERICAN GUILD OF
AUTHORS & COMPOSERS

Authorized for use by..

....

under agreement dated............................19.............. and Not Valid
Unless Countersigned by AGAC

UNIFORM POPULAR SONGWRITERS CONTRACT

Copyright ©1948 Songwriters Protective Ass'n.
Copyright ©1969 AGAC.

AGREEMENT made this day of , 19 , between

....

(hereinafter called "Publisher") and..

....

Jointly and/or severally hereinafter collectively called "Writer");

WITNESSETH:

Composition 1. The Writer hereby sells, assigns, transfers and delivers to the Publisher a certain heretofore unpublished original musical composition, written and/or composed by the above-named Writer now entitled

(hereinafter referred to as "the composition"), including the title, words and music thereof, and the right to secure copyright therein throughout the entire world, and to have and to hold the said copyright and all rights of whatsoever nature thereunder existing, for the original term of the United States copyright or for the period of twenty-eight years from the date of publication in the United States, whichever may be shorter, and subject to the terms of this contract.

Performing Rights Affiliation 2. In all respects this contract shall be subject to any existing agreements between any of the parties hereto and the small performing rights licensing organization of which Writer is a member or an affiliate.

Warranty 3. The Writer hereby warrants that the composition is his sole, exclusive and original work, that he has full right and power to make the within contract, and that there exists no adverse claim to or in the composition, except as aforesaid in Paragraph 2 hereof and except such rights as are specifically set forth in Paragraph 23 hereof.

Royalties 4. In consideration of this contract, the Publisher agrees to pay the Writer as follows:

Advance (a) $.....................as an advance against royalties, receipt of which is hereby acknowledged, which sum shall remain the property of the Writer and shall be deductible only from payments hereafter becoming due the Writer under this contract.

Piano Copies (b) In respect of regular piano copies sold and paid for in the United States and Canada, a royalty per copy according to whichever one of the following provisions is checked:

Fixed Royalty ☐ (i) ....¢ (in no case less than 3¢ per copy.)

Sliding Scale ☐ (ii) ....% (in no case, however, less than 11½%) of the wholesale selling price of the first 100,000 copies or less, but in no event less than 2¼¢ per copy; plus

........% (in no case, however, less than 14%) of the wholesale selling price of copies in excess of 100,000 and not exceeding 200,000, but in no event less than 3¢ per copy; plus

........% (in no case, however, less than 16%) of the wholesale selling price of copies in excess of 200,000 and not exceeding 300,000, but in no event less than 3½¢ per copy; plus

........% (in no case, however, less than 18%) of the wholesale selling price of copies in excess of 300,000 and not exceeding 400,000, but in no event less than 4¢ per copy; plus

........% (in no case, however, less than 20½%) of the wholesale selling price of copies in excess of 400,000 and not exceeding 500,000, but in no event less than 4½¢ per copy; plus

........% (in no case, however, less than 23%) of the wholesale selling price of all copies in excess of 500,000, but in no event less than 5¢ per copy.

Foreign Royalties (c) ....% (in no case, however, less than 50%) of all net sums received by the Publisher in respect of regular piano copies, orchestrations, band arrangements, octavos, quartets, arrangements for combinations of voices and/or instruments, and/or other copies of the composition sold in any country other than the United States and Canada, provided, however, that if the Publisher should sell such copies through, or cause them to be sold by, a subsidiary or affiliate which is actually doing business in a foreign country, then in respect of such sales, the Publisher shall pay to the Writer not less than 5% of the marked retail selling price in respect of each such copy sold and paid for.

Orchestrations and Other Arrangements, etc. (d) ....% (in no case, however, less than 10%) of the wholesale selling price (after trade discounts if any) of each copy sold and paid for in the United States and Canada, or for export from the United States, of orchestrations, band arrangements, octavos, quartets, arrangements for combinations of voices and/or instruments, and/or other copies of the composition (other than regular piano copies).

Publisher's Song Book, Song Sheet, Folio, etc. (e) (i) If the composition, or any part thereof, is included in any song book, song sheet, folio or similar publication issued by the Publisher containing at least four, but not more than twenty-five musical compositions, the royalty to be paid by the Publisher to the Writer shall be an amount determined by dividing 10% of the wholesale selling price (after trade discounts, if any) of the copies sold, among the total number of the Publisher's copyrighted musical compositions included in such publication. If such publication contains more than twenty-five musical compositions, the said 10% shall be increased by an additional ½% for each additional musical composition. The composition shall not, however, be included in any such publication earlier than six months after the date on which regular piano copies of the composition shall have been published, except that said six months period may be reduced to three months with the Writer's written consent given at any time after the expiration of three months.

Licensee's Song Book, Song Sheet, Folio, etc. (ii) If, pursuant to a license granted by the Publisher to a licensee not controlled by or affiliated with it, the composition, or any part thereof, is included in any song book, song sheet, folio or similar publication, containing at least four musical compositions, the royalty to be paid by the Publisher to the Writer shall be that proportion of 50% of the gross amount received by it from the licensee, as the number of uses of the composition under the license and during the license period, bears to the total number of uses of the Publisher's copyrighted musical compositions under the license and during the license period. The lyrics alone of the composition may be included in such a publication at any time, but the lyrics and music thereof, in combination, shall not be included earlier than two years after the date on which regular piano copies of the composition shall have been published. Such royalties shall be computed and paid within 30 days after the expiration of the term of each license, but if any such license term is in excess of one year, such royalties shall be computed and paid annually.

(iii) In computing the number of the Publisher's copyrighted musical compositions under subdivisions (i) and (ii) hereof, there shall be excluded musical compositions in the public domain and arrangements thereof and those with respect to which the Publisher does not currently publish and offer for sale regular piano copies.

(iv) Royalties on publications containing less than four musical compositions shall be payable at regular piano copy rates.

Professional Material and Free Copies (f) As to "professional material" not sold or resold, no royalty shall be payable. Free copies of the lyrics of the composition shall not be distributed except under the following conditions: (i) with the Writer's written consent; or (ii) when printed without music in limited numbers for charitable, religious or governmental purposes, or for similar public purposes, if no profit is derived, directly or indirectly; or (iii) when authorized for printing in a book, magazine or periodical, where such use is incidental to a novel or story (as distinguished from use in a book of lyrics or a lyric magazine or folio), provided that any such use shall bear the Writer's name and the proper copyright notice; or (iv) when distributed solely for the purpose of exploiting the composition, provided, that such exploitation is restricted to the distribution of limited numbers of such copies for the purpose of influencing the sale of the composition, that the distribution is independent of the sale of any other musical compositions, services, goods, wares or merchandise, and that no profit is made, directly or indirectly, in connection therewith.

Mechanicals, Electrical Transcription, Synchronization, All Other Rights (g) ....% (in no case, however, less than 50%) of:

All gross receipts of the Publisher in respect of any licenses (including statutory royalties) authorizing the manufacture of parts of instruments serving to mechanically reproduce the composition or to use the composition in synchronization with sound motion pictures, or to reproduce it upon electrical transcription for broadcasting purposes; and of any and all gross receipts of the Publisher from any other source or right now known or which may hereafter come into existence, except as provided in subdivision (i) of this paragraph 4.

Licensing Agent's Charges (h) If the Publisher administers licenses authorizing the manufacture of parts of instruments serving to mechanically reproduce said composition, or the use of said composition in synchronization or in timed relation with sound motion pictures or its reproduction upon electrical transcriptions, or any of them, through an agent, trustee or other administrator acting for a substantial part of the industry and not under the exclusive control of the Publisher (hereinafter sometimes referred to as licensing agent), the Publisher, in determining his receipts, shall be entitled to deduct from gross license fees paid by the Licensees, a sum equal to the charges paid by the Publisher to said licensing agent, provided, however, that in respect to synchronization or timed relation with sound motion pictures, said deduction shall in no event exceed $150.00 or 10% of said gross license fee, whichever is less; in connection with the manufacture of parts of instruments serving to mechanically reproduce said composition, said deductions shall not exceed 2½% of said gross license fee; and in connection with electrical transcriptions, said deductions shall not exceed 10% of said gross license fee.

Small Performing Royalties (i) Nothing contained in this agreement shall alter, vary or modify the rights of Writer and Publisher to share in, receive and retain the proceeds distributed to them by the small performing rights licensing organization (i.e., ...
of which both Writer and Publisher are members or affiliated pursuant to their respective agreements with such small performing rights licensing organization.

Block Licenses (j) The Publisher agrees that the use of the composition will not be included in any bulk or block license heretofore or hereafter granted, and that it will not grant any bulk or block license to include the same, without the written consent of American Guild of Authors and Composers on behalf of the Writer in each instance, except (i) that the Publisher may grant such licenses with respect to electrical transcription for broadcasting purposes, but in such event, the Publisher shall pay to the Writer that proportion of 50% of the gross amount received by it under each such license as the number of uses of the composition under each such license during each such license period bears to the total number of uses of the Publisher's copyrighted musical compositions under each such license during each such license period; in computing the number of the Publisher's copyrighted musical compositions for this purpose, there shall be excluded musical compositions in the public domain and arrangements thereof and those with respect to which the Publisher does not currently publish and offer for sale regular piano copies; and with respect to such licenses, the Publisher shall account to the Writer annually; (ii) that the Publisher may appoint agents or representatives in countries outside of the United States and Canada to use and to grant licenses for the use of the composition on the customary royalty fee basis under which the Publisher shall receive not less than 10% of the marked retail selling price in respect of regular piano copies, and 50% of all other revenue; if, in connection with any such bulk or block license, the Publisher shall have received any advance, the Writer shall not be entitled to share therein, but no part of said advance shall be deducted in computing the composition's earnings under said bulk or block license. A bulk or block license shall be deemed to mean any license or agreement, domestic or foreign, whereby rights are granted in respect of two or more musical compositions.

Television and New Uses (k) Except to the extent that the Publisher and Writer have heretofore or may hereafter assign to or vest in the small performing rights licensing organization of which Writer is a member or an affiliate, the said rights or the right to grant licenses therefor, it is agreed that no licenses shall be granted without the written consent, in each instance, of the Writer for the use of the composition by means of television, or by any means, or for any purposes not commercially established, or for which licenses were not granted by the Publisher on musical compositions prior to June 1, 1937.

Writer's Consent to Licenses (l) The Publisher shall not, without the written consent of the Writer in each case, give or grant any right or license (i) to use the title of the composition, or (ii) for the exclusive use of the composition in any form or for any purpose, or for any period of time, or for any territory, other than its customary arrangements with foreign publishers, or (iii) to give a dramatic representation of the composition or to dramatize the plot or story thereof, or (iv) for a vocal rendition of the composition in synchronization with sound motion pictures, or (v) for any synchronization use thereof after the expiration of ten years from the date on which regular piano copies of the composition shall have been first published, or (vi) for the use of the composition or a quotation or excerpt therefrom in any article, book, periodical, advertisement or other similar publication. If, however, the Publisher shall give to the Writer written notice, by registered mail or telegram, specifying the right or license to be given or granted, the name of the licensee and the terms and conditions thereof, including the price or other compensation to be received therefor, then, unless the Writer (or any one or more of them) shall, within seventy-two hours (exclusive of Saturdays, Sundays and holidays) after the delivery of such notice to the address of the Writer hereinafter designated, object thereto, the Publisher may grant such right or license in accordance with the said notice without first obtaining the consent of the Writer. Such notice shall be deemed sufficient if sent to the Writer at the address or addresses hereinafter designated or at the address or addresses last furnished to the Publisher in writing by the Writer.

Trust for Writer (m) Any portion of the receipts which may become due to the Writer from license fees (in excess of offsets), whether received directly from the licensee or from any licensing agent of the Publisher, shall, if not paid immediately on the receipt thereof by the Publisher, belong to the Writer and shall be held in trust for the Writer until payment is made; the ownership of said trust fund by the Writer shall not be questioned whether the monies are physically segregated or not.

Writer Participation (n) The Publisher agrees that it will not issue any license as a result of which it will receive any financial benefit in which the Writer does not participate.

Writer Credit (o) Every license or authorization issued by the Publisher authorizing the publication of the composition or any part thereof shall contain a provision requiring the user thereof to print, in addition to the copyright notice, the name of the Writer as the author thereof.

Change in Piano Copy Royalty (p) If a fixed royalty is designated to be payable with respect to regular piano copies of the composition (as provided in paragraph 4 (b) (i), then, if at any time, the Publisher shall increase or decrease the wholesale selling price which it charged on January 1, 1947 to regular music jobbers for regular piano copies of musical compositions of the same class or category as the composition, then the said fixed royalty shall be increased or decreased in proportion to the change in said wholesale selling price.

Writers' Respective Shares 5. Whenever the term "Writer" is used herein, it shall be deemed to mean all of the persons named herein below, and any and all royalties herein provided to be paid to the Writer shall be paid jointly to the following persons if there be more than one, and shall be divided among them as follows:

Name	Share
....	....
....	....
....	....
....	....

Publication 6. (a) The Publisher shall, within one year from the date hereof, make, publish and offer for sale regular piano copies of the composition in the form and through the channels customarily employed by it for that purpose, and in addition, either (i) cause a commercial phonograph recording to be made and distributed in the customary form and through the customary commercial channels, or (ii) make, publish and offer for sale a dance orchestra arrangement. As an alternative to compliance with (i) or (ii), the Publisher shall pay to the Writer the sum of $250.00 less the aggregate of any advances paid, as stated in Paragraph 4 (a) hereof, and any royalties paid to the Writer within said one-year period. If, in the statement of "Special Exceptions" hereinafter set forth, the composition shall have been designated as one which is not intended for publication in regular piano copies, the Publisher shall be deemed to have complied with this paragraph by the making and distribution of a commercial phonograph recording and either the publication of a dance orchestra arrangement or the payment of the $250.00, all as aforesaid.

Failure to Publish (b) Should the Publisher fail to comply with the provisions of subdivision (a) hereof, the Writer shall be entitled to demand in writing the return of the composition at any time after the expiration of said year, whereupon the Publisher must, within one month after the receipt of such notice, either comply with the provisions of subdivision (a) hereof, in which event this contract will remain in full force and effect, or upon its failure so to comply, this contract shall terminate and all rights of any and every nature in and to the composition and in and to any and all copyrights secured thereon in the United States and throughout the world, shall re-vest in and become the property of the Writer and shall be reassigned to him by the Publisher; the Writer shall not be obligated to return or pay to the Publisher any advance or indebtedness as a condition of such re-assignment; the said re-assignment shall be in accordance with and subject to the provisions of Paragraph 13 hereof, and in addition, the Publisher shall pay to the Writer all gross sums which it has theretofore or may thereafter receive in respect of the composition.

Writer's Copies (c) The Publisher shall furnish the Writer copies of the composition which it publishes and shall use its best efforts to furnish or cause to be furnished to the Writer copies published by others.

Foreign Copyright 7. (a) Each copyright on the composition in countries other than the United States shall be secured only in the name of the Publisher, and the Publisher shall not at any time divest itself of said foreign copyright directly or indirectly, except to the extent that it may be obligated to do so by virtue of an agreement entered into by the Publisher with a foreign publisher prior to January 1, 1947, and then only for the term of said agreement.

Foreign Publication (b) Except to the extent that the Publisher is obligated to a foreign publisher or licensee by written agreement made prior to January 1, 1947, and then only for the term of said agreement, no rights shall be granted by the Publisher in the composition to any foreign publisher or licensee inconsistent with the terms hereof, nor shall any foreign publication rights in the composition be given to a foreign publisher or licensee unless and until the Publisher shall have complied with the provisions of Paragraph 6 hereof.

Foreign Advance (c) If foreign rights in the composition are separately conveyed, otherwise than as a part of the Publisher's current and/or future catalog, not less than 50% of any advance received in respect thereof shall be credited to the account of and paid to the Writer.

Foreign Percentage (d) The percentage of the Writer on monies received from foreign sources shall be computed on the Publisher's net receipts, provided, however, that no deductions shall be made for offsets of monies due from the Publisher to said foreign sources; or for advances made by such foreign sources to the Publisher, unless the Writer shall have received at least 50% of said advances.

No Foreign Allocations (e) In computing the receipts of the Publisher from licenses granted in respect of synchronization with sound motion pictures, or in respect of any world-wide licenses, or in respect of licenses granted by the Publisher for use of the composition in countries other than the United States, no amount shall be deducted for payments or allocations to publishers or licensees in such countries.

Terms of Contract 8. All rights in and to the composition and any copyrights secured thereon throughout the world, shall revert to the Writer upon expiration of the original term of the United States copyright or at the end of twenty-eight (28) years from the date of publication in the United States, whichever period shall be shorter. The Publisher shall, at the expiration of said period, execute any and all documents which may be necessary or proper to re-vest in the Writer any and all rights in and to the composition and in and to any copyright in the United States or any other countries throughout the world; provided, however, that if the Writer shall sell or assign to some person other than the Publisher, his rights in the United States renewal copyright in the composition, or any of his rights in the composition in the United States or elsewhere, for the period beyond said original term or twenty-eight years, as the case may be, then, unless there shall have been given to the Publisher at least six months' written notice of an intention to offer said rights for sale, the Publisher shall not be obligated to assign to the Writer said rights in countries other than the United States and Canada, and this contract, and the assignment under Paragraph 1 hereof, shall all continue in respect of such rights in countries other than the United States and Canada.

Negotiations for New or Unspecified Uses 9. If the Publisher desires to exercise a right in and to the composition now known or which may hereafter become known, but for which no specific provision has been made herein, the Publisher shall give written notice to the Writer thereof. Negotiations respecting all the terms and conditions of any such disposition shall thereupon be entered into between the Publisher (and/or the National Music Publishers' Association, Inc.) and the American Guild of Authors & Composers; and no such right shall be exercised until specific agreement has been made.

Royalty Statements and Payments 10. The Publisher shall render to the Writer, hereafter, royalty statements accompanied by remittance of the amount due on or before, each May 15th covering the 3 months ending March 31st; each August 15th covering the 3 months ending June 30th; each November 15th covering the 3 months ending September 30th; each February 15th covering the 3 months ending December 31st; provided, however, that if it shall have heretofore been the custom of the Publisher to render royalty statements accompanied by remittance of the amount due semi-annually, or quarterly at the end of different quarterly periods, such custom may be continued. The Writer may at any time, or from time to time, make written request for a detailed royalty statement, and the Publisher shall, within sixty days, comply therewith. Such royalty statements shall set forth in detail the various items, foreign and domestic, for which royalties are payable thereunder and the amounts thereof, including, but not limited to, the number of copies sold and the number of uses made in each royalty category. If a use is made in a publication of the character provided in Paragraph 4, subdivision (e) hereof, there shall be included in said royalty statement the title of said publication, the publisher or issuer thereof, the date of and number of uses, the gross license fee received in connection with each publication, the share thereto of all the writers under contract with the Publisher, and the Writer's share thereof. There shall likewise be included in said statement a description of every other use of the composition, and if by a licensee or licensees their name or names, and if said use is upon a part of an instrument serving to reproduce the composition mechanically, the type of mechanical reproduction, the title of the label thereon, the name or names of the artists performing the same, together with the gross license fees received, and the Writer's share thereof.

Examination of Books 11. (a) The Publisher shall from time to time, upon written demand of the Writer or his representative, permit the Writer or his representative to inspect at the place of business of the Publisher, all books, records and documents relating to the composition and all licenses granted, uses had and payments made therefor, such right of inspection to include, but not by way of limitation, the right to examine all original accountings and records relating to uses and payments by manufacturers of commercial phonograph records and music rolls; and the Writer or his representative may appoint a certified public accountant who shall at any time during usual business hours have access to all records of the Publisher relating to the composition for the purpose of verifying royalty statements rendered or which are delinquent under the terms hereof.

(b) The Publisher shall, upon written demand of the Writer or his representative, cause any licensing agent in the United States and Canada to furnish to the Writer or his representative, statements showing in detail all licenses granted, uses had and payments made in connection with the composition, which licenses or permits were granted, or payments were received, by or through said licensing agent, and to permit the Writer or his representative to inspect at the place of business of such licensing agent, all books, records and documents of such licensing agent, relating thereto. Any and all agreements made by the Publisher with any such licensing agent shall provide that any such licensing agent will comply with the terms and provisions hereof. In the event that the Publisher shall instruct such licensing agent to furnish to the Writer or his representative statements as provided for herein, and to permit the inspection of the books, records and documents as herein provided, then if such licensing agent should refuse to comply with the said instructions, or any of them, the Publisher agrees to institute and prosecute diligently and in good faith such action or proceedings as may be necessary to compel compliance with the said instructions.

(c) With respect to foreign licensing agents, the Publisher shall make available the books or records of said licensing agents in countries outside of the United States and Canada to the extent such books or records are available to the Publisher, except that the Publisher may in lieu thereof make available any accountants' reports and audits which the Publisher is able to obtain.

Default in Payment or Prevention of Examination 12. If the Publisher shall fail or refuse, within sixty days after written demand, to furnish or cause to be furnished, such statements, books, records or documents, or to permit inspection thereof, as provided for in Paragraphs 10 and 11 hereof, or within thirty days after written demand, to make the payment of any royalties due under this contract, then the Writer shall have the option, to be exercised upon ten days' written notice, to terminate this contract. However, if the Publisher shall:

(a) Within the said ten-day period:

(i) serve upon the Writer a written notice demanding arbitration; and

(ii) if the demand be for statements, books, records or documents, or to permit inspection thereof, deposit with National Music Publishers' Association, Inc. a re-assignment to the Writer of the copyright and all other rights in and to the composition, to be held in escrow pending the determination of the arbitration, or if the demand be for royalties, then deposit in escrow with National Music Publishers' Association, Inc., the amount shown by its books to be due the Writer under the provisions of this contract; and,

(b) Submit to arbitration its claim that it has complied with its obligation to furnish statements, books, records or documents, or permitted inspection thereof, or to pay royalties, as the case may be, or both, and thereafter comply with any award of the arbitrators within ten days after such award or within such time as the arbitrators may specify;

then this contract shall continue in full force and effect as if the Writer's option had not been exercised. But if the Publisher shall fail to comply with the foregoing provisions, then this contract shall be deemed to have been terminated as of the date of the Writer's exercise of his option to terminate this contract.

Termination of Contract 13. Upon the termination of this contract, all rights of any and every nature in and to the composition and in and to any and all copyrights secured thereon in the United States and throughout the world, shall re-vest in and become the property of the Writer, and shall be re-assigned to the Writer by the Publisher free of any and all encumbrances of any nature whatsoever, provided that:

(a) The said re-assignment by the Publisher may, however, be subject to such rights, if any, as may have been vested in a foreign publisher respecting the use of the composition in countries other than the United States and Canada under any agreement made prior to January 1, 1947.

(b) If the Publisher, prior to such termination, shall have granted a domestic license for the use of the composition, not inconsistent with the terms and provisions of this contract, the re-assignment may be subject to the terms of such license.

(c) In either of the events mentioned in subdivisions (a) and (b) of this paragraph, however, the Publisher shall assign to the Writer all rights which it may have under any such agreement or license in respect of the composition, including, but not limited to, the right to receive all royalties or other monies earned by the composition thereunder after the date of termination of this contract. Should the Publisher thereafter receive or be credited with any royalties or other monies so earned, it shall pay the same to the Writer.

(d) The Writer shall not be obligated to return or pay to the Publisher any advance or indebtedness as a condition of the re-assignment provided for in this Paragraph 13, and shall be entitled to receive the plates and copies of the composition in the possession of the Publisher.

(e) The termination of this contract shall not relieve the Publisher of his obligation to pay any and all royalties which may have accrued to the Writer prior to such termination.

(f) The Publisher shall execute any and all documents and do any and all acts or things necessary to effect any and all re-assignments to the Writer herein provided for.

Notices 14. All written demands and notices provided for herein shall be sent by registered mail.

Suits for Infringement 15. Any legal action brought by the Publisher against any alleged infringer of the composition shall be initiated and prosecuted at its sole cost and expense, but if the Publisher should fail, within thirty days after written demand, to institute such action, the Writer shall be entitled to institute such suit at his cost and expense. All sums recovered as a result of any such action shall, after the deduction of the reasonable expense thereof, be divided equally between the Publisher and the Writer. No settlement of any such action may be made by either party without first notifying the other; in the event that either party should object to such settlement, then such settlement shall not be made if the party objecting assumes the prosecution of the action and all expenses thereof, except that any sums thereafter recovered shall be divided equally between the Publisher and the Writer after the deduction of the reasonable expenses thereof.

Infringement Claims 16. (a) If a claim is presented against the Publisher alleging that the composition is an infringement upon some other work or a violation of any other right of another, and because thereof the Publisher is jeopardized, it shall forthwith serve a written notice upon the Writer setting forth the full details of such claim. The pendency of said claim shall not relieve the Publisher of the obligation to make payment of the royalties to the Writer hereunder, unless the Publisher shall deposit said royalties as and when they would otherwise be payable, in an account in a bank or trust company in the City of New York in the joint names of the Publisher and the Writer. If no suit be filed within nine months after said written notice from the Publisher to the Writer, all monies deposited in said joint account shall be paid over to the Writer plus any interest which may have been earned thereon.

(b) Should an action be instituted against the Publisher claiming that the composition is an infringement upon some other work or a violation of any other right of another, the Publisher shall forthwith serve written notice upon the Writer containing the full details of such claim. Notwithstanding the commencement of such action, the Publisher shall continue to pay the royalties hereunder to the Writer unless it shall, from and after the date of the service of the summons, deposit said royalties as and when they would otherwise be payable, in an account in a bank or trust company in the City of

New York in the joint names of the Publisher and the Writer. If the said suit shall be finally adjudicated in favor of the Publisher or shall be settled, there shall be released and paid to the Writer all of such sums held in escrow less any amount paid out of the Writer's share with the Writer's written consent in settlement of said action. Should the said suit finally result adversely to the Publisher, the said amount on deposit shall be released to the Publisher to the extent of any expense or damage it incurs and the balance shall be paid over to the Writer.

(c) In any of the foregoing events, however, the Writer shall be entitled to payment of said royalties or the money so deposited at and after such time as he files with the Publisher a surety company bond, or a bond in other form acceptable to the Publisher, in the sum of such payments to secure the return thereof to the extent that the Publisher may be entitled to such return. The foregoing payments or deposits or the filing of a bond shall be without prejudice to the rights of the Publisher or Writer in the premises.

Arbitration

17. Any and all differences, disputes or controversies arising out of this contract shall be submitted to arbitration under the laws of the State of New York, and the parties hereby individually and jointly agree to abide by and perform any award rendered in such arbitration, and agree that a judgment of the Supreme Court of the State of New York may be entered upon such award. Together with the demand for arbitration, the party making said demand shall designate an arbitrator and the adverse party shall, within ten days thereafter, likewise designate an arbitrator. The two arbitrators so chosen shall promptly appoint a third arbitrator who shall act as Chairman and any award concurred in by a majority of the arbitrators shall be binding upon the parties. Should the party against whom arbitration is demanded fail to select an arbitrator, or should the arbitrators selected by the parties be unable to agree upon a third arbitrator, then said arbitrator or arbitrators, as the case may be, shall be designated and appointed in the manner provided by the Arbitration Law of the State of New York.

Assignment

18. Except to the extent herein otherwise expressly provided, the Publisher shall not sell, transfer, assign, convey, encumber or otherwise dispose of the composition or the copyright or copyrights secured thereon without the prior written consent of the Writer. The Writer has been induced to enter into this contract in reliance upon the value to him of the personal service and ability of the Publisher in the exploitation of the composition, and by reason thereof it is the intention of the parties and the essence of the relationship between them that the rights herein granted to the Publisher shall remain with the Publisher and that the same shall not pass to any other person, including, without limitations, successors to or receivers or trustees of the property of the Publisher, either by act or deed of the Publisher or by operation of law, and in the event of the voluntary or involuntary bankruptcy of the Publisher, this contract shall terminate, provided, however, that the composition may be included by the Publisher in a bona fide voluntary sale of its music business or its entire catalog of musical compositions, or in a merger or consolidation of the Publisher with another corporation; and provided further that the composition and the copyright therein may be assigned by the Publisher to a subsidiary or affiliated company generally engaged in the music publishing business. If the Publisher is an individual, the composition may pass to a legatee or distributee as part of the inheritance of the Publisher's music business and entire catalog of musical compositions. Any such transfer or assignment shall, however, be conditioned upon the execution and delivery by the transferee or assignee to the Writer of an agreement to be bound by and to perform all of the terms and conditions of this contract to be performed on the part of the Publisher.

Subsidiary Defined

19. A subsidiary, affiliate, or any person, firm or corporation controlled by the Publisher or by such subsidiary or affiliate, as used in this contract, shall be deemed to include any person, firm or corporation, under common control with, or the majority of whose stock or capital contribution is owned or controlled by the Publisher or by any of its officers, directors, partners or associates, or whose policies and actions are subject to domination or control by the Publisher or any of its officers, directors, partners or associates.

Minimums

20. The minimum amounts and percentages specified in this contract shall be deemed to be the amounts and percentages agreed upon by the parties hereto, unless greater amounts or percentages are inserted in the blank spaces provided therefor.

Countersignature and Modifications

21. This contract is binding upon and shall enure to the benefit of the parties hereto and their respective successors in interest (as hereinbefore limited), but shall be effective only when countersigned by the American Guild of Authors & Composers. If the Writer (or one or more of them) shall not be living, any notices may be given to, or consents given by, his or their successors in interest. No change or modification of this contract shall be effective unless reduced to writing, signed by the parties hereto, and countersigned by the American Guild of Authors & Composers.

Marginal Notes

22. The marginal notes are inserted only as a matter of convenience and for reference, and in no way define, limit or describe the scope or intent of this contract nor in any way affect this contract.

Exceptions to Warranties

23. The rights specifically excepted, as provided in Paragraph 3 hereof are as follows:

Witness: ....

....

Witness: ....

....

Witness: ....

....

Witness: ....

Publisher ....

By ....

Address ....

Writer .... (L.S.)

Address ....

Writer .... (L.S.)

Address ....

Writer .... (L.S.)

AMERICAN GUILD OF AUTHORS & COMPOSERS
formerly
Countersigned: **SONGWRITERS PROTECTIVE ASSOCIATION**

Address ....

By: ....

* * * * *

Special Exceptions to apply only if filled in and initialed by the parties.

☐ (a) The composition is:

☐ Standard   ☐ Pastoral
☐ Secular   ☐ Instrumental

and the Publisher is not required to publish piano copies or otherwise comply with the provisions of Paragraph 6.

☐ (b) The composition is one of a number of musical compositions delivered to the Publisher by the Writer under an agreement dated _____, a copy of which is hereto annexed. Unless a shorter period is stated in the annexed agreement, the Writer shall not be entitled to demand the return of the composition for the Publisher's failure to publish regular piano copies or otherwise with the provisions of Paragraph 6, until five years after the expiration of the said annexed agreement.

☐ (c) The composition is part of an original score (not an interpolation) of

☐ Living Stage Production   ☐ Motion Picture   ☐ Night Club Revue

which is the subject of an agreement between the parties dated _____, a copy of which is hereto annexed. Unless said agreement requires compliance with Paragraph 6 in respect of a greater number of musical compositions, the Publisher shall be deemed to have complied with said Paragraph 6 with respect to the composition if it fully performs the terms of said Paragraph 6 in respect of any one musical composition included in said score.

☐ (d) The composition is not one intended to be published in regular piano copies.

14: How to Become Your Own Music Publisher

SONGWRITERS, for any of the reasons listed below, often inquire into the mechanics of publishing their own music. Because of such widespread requests or in hope of giving songwriters greater insight into the complex world of music publishing, a procedure for starting and running a music publishing company will be offered. It should be stated, however obvious, that any explanation of this process will be oversimplified. The real learning of how to become a music publisher comes from the actual operation.

Why a Songwriter Starts a Publishing Company

A songwriter will become a music publisher for any of the following reasons:

1. His songs have been rejected by all publishing companies he has submitted them to.
2. He wants to control his own copyrights.
3. He feels he can do a better job for his songs than other publishers.
4. He believes there is substantial potential income from his songs and wishes to collect the publishing revenue himself.
5. He believes that if his songs are good enough to be accepted

by an ''outside'' publisher, then they are worth his efforts to publish them himself.

6. He has acquired sufficient knowledge and experience in the music business to place and publish his songs himself.

Starting Your Own Music Publishing Company

Decide on a name for your company. Check with ASCAP, BMI, or SESAC to make sure the name you select doesn't conflict with an existing publishing company of the same name. Affiliation with a performing rights organization comes at a later point.

Obtain a business permit. Local business laws may require you to register your company as a business enterprise. Check with the city clerk or city hall. It is highly recommended you consult an attorney when doing this.

Copyright your songs (see chapter 4 for a detailed explanation).

Print business stationery. Since you will be corresponding by mail frequently, print stationery including your company name, address, and telephone number.

Make your demos as good as possible. The final determination regarding acceptance of your song will be based upon the listener's evaluation of the song itself. Your song will be in competition with several lavishly produced demos and a poor representation of your song might, ashamedly so, be the factor that gets your song rejected.

Placing your song. The ability of an experienced publisher to place a song and the lack of it by the newcomer is often the argument of those who oppose songwriters becoming their own publishers. Financial and copyright administration is all academic, they say, but the knowledge of the record market, finesse, and personal relationships built up over the years are the ingredients that make for a successful publisher.

The fact is, while that is true to an extent, these ''ingredients'' are not necessary to the degree often stressed. If your song is good enough, that is, if it's ''in the grooves,'' you, as its publisher, can place it.

You should study the singles charts in the trades religiously. Determine which of these chart-making artists would be compatible for your songs and audition them for these people by submitting the material to their record company, producer, agent, or manager by appointment or by mail. (Addresses and telephone numbers can be found from several of the sources listed in chapter 6.) If you mail your material, send a maximum of four songs, with a typed letter on business stationery, a lead sheet, and a self-addressed stamped envelope.

Keep details of your efforts. The following method is a recommended means for you to keep details of your efforts as a publisher: have three sets of 3 x 5 index cards on file. Designate set one "songs"; set two "artists"; set three "record companies, producers, managers, etc." In your "songs" card file, list alphabetically all the songs in your catalog, or those which you are actively working with, each song title on a separate card. Indicate to whom you sent copies of that song, when, and responses, if any. Under your "artists" file, have a separate card naming each recording artist to whom you recommended a song, along with the person's name to whom you sent it. For the "record companies, producers, managers, etc." file, make a separate card for each company or individual you sent a demo to, including the name, address, and telephone number, and the date sent and response, if any.

Keeping records of your efforts in this manner is very practical. It permits you to study each file separately, which may result in your discovery of a potential artist, producer, or record company you forgot to send your songs to.

Affiliate with a performing rights organization. At the time an artist or producer notifies you that your song is going to be recorded or performed, select and apply to one of the performing rights organizations for publisher affiliation (see chapter 10).

Affiliate with a mechanical rights organization. At the time an artist or producer notifies you that your song is going to be recorded, contact a mechanical rights organization to administer and collect mechanical license fees for recordings of your compositions. You may decide to affiliate with a mechanical rights organization that performs other duties, such as administer synchronization licenses or register copyrights with the Copyright Office (see chapter 11).

Once your song has been recorded and released, you will want to increase the song's potential income by doing the following:

Arrange to have an independent sheet music printing company

print and distribute copies of your song if it is released as a single and achieves a certain degree of success.

Try to obtain cover records. Use the version just recorded as your "demo" and send this around to artists who might be suitable to record your song.

Acquire foreign representation. You will want to acquire foreign representation of your song whereby artists in other countries would have a record of your song out in their market. By contacting various publishers (there are references to these in the trades and annual directories) you can try to reach an agreement with a foreign publisher to "subpublish" your song. Your company and the subpublisher will split the profits for his territory. Sometimes foreign lyrics will have to be written which might alter the terms of the deal.

The more successful your song is in the United States, the better your chances to acquire a subpublisher to represent it. Many foreign publishers will not represent a song in their territory unless it is a hit in the United States, or they feel it has great potential for their territory. In other words, the mere fact that your song has been recorded, even if by a name artist, does not mean it will be subpublished in other countries.

Maintain copyright administration. You must maintain proper administration of your copyright. Improper copyright administration may result in loss of revenue or your songs going into the public domain. If you are too busy in your creative capacities to maintain proper administration, you might contact a major publishing company or one of the mechanical rights organizations that handles copyright administration to do this for you. If you are building up a catalog of recorded songs, they will be interested in handling these administrations for a certain percentage of your gross receipts.

Before you decide to start your own publishing company, you should be fully aware that there is financial risk involved. A publisher's expenses can run high. He assumes telephone, mailing, promotion, and demo expenses, among others, without the guarantee that his song will even be recorded. Before deciding to start your own publishing company, you should fully investigate your financial resources and objectively examine if this move is in your best interests.

15: Making Your Own Masters and Selling Them

A MASTER IS a finished tape recording of a song from which records are pressed and distributed to radio stations and record stores.

Producing Your Own Master

Songwriters feel strongly about their work. Many believe that if their best tunes were recorded and presented to the public, there would be a good chance they would have a "hit," or at least a money-maker. The songwriter who decides to produce his own record does so because of any of the following reasons: his song has been rejected by all parties who have auditioned it; he cannot reach the artist for whom he wishes to audition his song; there is no recording artist he can think of for whom his song would be compatible; he believes in his ability to produce the song into a commercial record; or he is part of a group that wishes to do their own production.

If you decide to take this venture upon yourself, do so only if you can afford the financial losses you might incur. You are speculating because you believe in the potential of your product, but by no means is there any guarantee a record company will purchase your master. One major record company executive says: "There are a lot of *good* masters floating around. If someone wants to sell one, their master has got to be *better* than good."

If, after you have carefully weighed the risk involved, you still wish to pursue this venture, make sure you know exactly what to do every step of the way.

As an independent producer, you must, of course, assume all the responsibilities of such. You must concern yourself with each of the following.

Selection of material. You might decide to record one song or a few. You should limit the production to your four best songs—and only if you believe each could stand up alone as a hit.

It might be in your best interests to take a demo of the material you are going to record to professionals in the music industry to get some feedback. They might tell you what potential, if any, your songs have, give you suggestions, or offer to attempt to sell the masters for you after they have been completed.

Selection of the artist. If you are producing yourself or a group of which you are a member, then you are not concerned with artist selection, except perhaps for back-up vocals. If, however, you are seeking an artist to record your material, be careful and selective. You must make sure that the artist you select is suited to sing your songs. A record company may like your songs, but pass up a deal because they didn't like the artist. Or they might find they have an artist similar to yours on their label. Such factors as the sex, age, and race of the artist will influence a record company's decision to purchase your masters. The artist's style is, of course, of paramount importance. A record company's final decision may be based upon its impression of whether or not the artist has a unique voice quality or vocal style that could be easily identified after his or her first release.

Selection of the producer. Although you are actually "producing" the session, by virtue of your financial backing, you should have an experienced record producer assume the creative capacities that will make the record commercial and competitive. You have probably had little or no experience in producing records, and therefore should not assume this role until you have had many hours of studio experience and are knowledgeable in all aspects of studio recording.

You should select a producer who is not only qualified but one who likes your material and is compatible for you to work with. As "executive producer" you are doing the hiring and have the right to choose whomever you wish. Since you will be working very closely with this person, it is imperative you both see eye to eye on all matters pertinent to the session and are capable of sustaining amiable relations with regard to the session at all times.

After you make your selection, you will enter into a coproduction agreement with the producer. That is, he will charge you a fee for his services and request a certain percentage of the production royalties. Fees normally range from $200 to $1,000 and the percentage will either be a specified amount determined before production, usually between 2 and 3½ percent, or be half the production points of whatever deal you may make with a record company. If, for instance, you make a deal with a label for nine points and give the artist three, you will have six points remaining. Your coproducer would therefore get three points and you would get three points. One point is equal to 1 percent of the retail list price of 90 percent of all records sold.

Using a producer with a track record might prove highly beneficial. Not only is he capable of producing a commercial record but his reputation might place you in a position to obtain a better production contract with a record company. And, of course, he has invaluable contacts that might assist you in placing the master with a label.

Selection of the arranger. Equal in importance to the selection of the producer is the selection of the arranger. Many producers are arrangers themselves or could recommend a competent one. If the producer you select is also the arranger, this latter expense will be absorbed into a total production fee.

Groups which are self-contained and produce and arrange their own material may wish to "sweeten" their tracks. If they cannot write the charts for these instruments (such as strings and horns), they should hire a competent individual who can (see chapter 9).

Rehearsal. Needless to say, the recording artist must rehearse the song until he can perform it to the best of his or her ability. Otherwise, unnecessary money will be spent on expensive studio time to get a final "take."

If the musical accompaniment will be performed by professional studio musicians, they will not rehearse prior to the session. They will sight-read the charts when they arrive, run through them a few times, and be ready to record. If you are part of a self-contained group, each member should have perfected his or her part before going into the studio.

The studio (and the engineer). You should permit the producer you hire to choose the studio you are going to record in. Of course, he will have to select one within the means of your budget, but considering your financial limitations, he will book the best quality studio you can afford. He might also have developed a good working relationship with the studio's engineer due to prior experience at that studio. However, it is not unusual for a producer to hire a free-lance engineer, one whom he has worked with previously and has much confidence in. A good engineer contributes more than the mere operation of machines. His skill in assisting the producer to obtain the best possible sounds and mix is one of the unheralded, yet vital, contributions essential for a successful record.

The production of masters on twenty-four-track equipment and tape is becoming more popular today than ever before. However, use of sixteen-track facilities is still most common and prices for sixteen-track studio time range in price from $125 to $200 per hour. The price might be slightly less expensive for mixing time.

Union sessions. The record industry is bound by conditions imposed upon it by two unions representing performers on recordings. These are the American Federation of Musicians (AF of M), which represents musicians (and arrangers, contractors and copyists), and the American Federation of Television and Radio Artists (AFTRA), which represents singers (and actors, announcers, narrators, and sound effects artists).

The recording and purchase of masters for release by a record company must be made within prescribed regulations set forth by the AF of M and AFTRA. These "codes" call for such things as a minimum payment for services rendered by the performer (affected by such factors as length of time in the studio, amount of overdubs, and performance of additional services such as conducting or coaching) and payment to the unions' pension and welfare funds.

It is not necessary that the musicians and vocalists on your master be members of the music union at the time the master is sold. The record company can purchase and release your master by paying the musicians the difference between what you paid them and the minimum union wage they would have earned under the AF of M's Phonograph Record Labor Agreement and by paying the vocalists the difference between what you paid them and the minimum union wage they would have earned under the AFTRA Code of Fair

Practice for Phonograph Recordings. From these wages, the musicians and vocalists are obliged to make the proper contribution to each union's pension and welfare funds. Henceforth, from the time of purchase, all recording dates will have to be union sessions. These same conditions apply to demos purchased by record companies and released as masters, where the participants were not members of the union.

Selling Your Master

Although the conditions upon which a record company may purchase your master have just been discussed, the "moment of truth" comes at the time you are attempting to sell your master. You should put the same care and meticulous planning into selling your record as you did into creating it. This consists of the following:

Artist representation. All record companies realize the importance in the development of a recording artist's career. They want to be assured the artist has a competent manager who will be able to promote and sustain the artist's growth as a performer and record seller. Likewise, the artist should have a booking agency or other agent assigned to schedule live performances for him.

Concert performances. The sales of records are augmented by live appearances by the artist. The record company is therefore concerned that the artist is effective when performing in front of large audiences and has access to a back-up band if not a member of a self-contained group. The artist must, of course, be available for lengthy tours to major cities across the nation and otherwise.

Biography and photos. The record company will wish to review the history and see a visual representation of the artist. If they develop sufficient interest, they might arrange for a personal interview or observe the artist making a local performance.

Check your tape or acetate. Don't submit a copy of your song that looks worn and has been subjected to repeated playings. The listener might feel you have been peddling a product that has been rejected by several others and this might leave a poor impression on your product before it is even played. Also, be sure to check for distortion in the tape or skips in the acetate.

Sale of Masters (Records) *

Date _____

Dear Sir :

    This letter will set forth and constitute a binding agreement between you (hereinafter referred to as "Seller") and ourselves (hereinafter referred to as "Purchaser").

    1.   (a)   Seller represents and warrants that it is the sole and exclusive owner of the entire right, title and interest including all copyrights and all property rights in and to the master recordings set forth in Schedule A, annexed hereto and made a part hereof, and in and to the performances embodied thereon for the entire world (hereinafter referred to as the "Masters").

    (b)   Seller further represents and warrants that the Masters and the performances embodied thereon were produced in all respects in accordance with the rules and regulations of the American Federation of Musicians and all other Unions having jurisdiction; that it has the entire right and authority to enter into and to perform this agreement and all parts thereof; that it has not granted, nor has it done or permitted others to do, nor will it do or permit others to do any acts or things which would be in derogation of the absolute title or any of the rights herein granted to Purchaser, nor has it made nor will it make any grant of rights or permit the making of any grant of rights incorporated with the title and rights herein granted to any one other than Purchaser; that there are no claims or threats of claims or litigations involving the Masters or said performances; that all costs incurred in the creation and production of such Master have been paid and that neither the Master nor the performances embodied thereon nor any use thereof by Purchaser or its grantees will violate or infringe upon the rights of any third parties. Seller agrees to and hereby does hold Purchaser harmless against any and all liability, loss, damage, cost or expense, including legal fees, paid by or incurred by reason of any breach or failure or claim of breach or failure of any of Seller's covenants, warranties or representations hereunder. Pending the determination of any such claim, failure or breach. Purchaser is granted the right to withhold payment of royalties hereunder.

    2.   Seller hereby sells, assigns and transfers to Purchaser, its successors or assigns, absolutely and forever and without any limitations or restrictions whatever, not specifically set forth herein, the entire right, title and interest in and to each of the Masters and in and to each of the performances embodied thereon. Promptly following the execution of this agreement Seller shall deliver to Purchaser all tape recordings, acetates and metal or other parts or reproductions of said masters presently in existence Seller further assigns to Purchaser absolutely and forever all rights and privileges of Seller to use the names, biographies and likenesses of all artists whose performances are embodied on said Masters, and all other rights, privileges and interests now known or hereafter to come into existence, now or here after owned or controlled by Seller, which pertain to, have any commercial affect upon or are derived from said Masters and the performances embodied thereon.

    3.   In full consideration for the sale to it of said Masters and of the performances embodied thereon, Purchaser agrees to pay to Seller :

    (a)   A sum equal to   percent of the retail list price (_____ cents per record) for ninety (90%) percent of all records manufactured from said Masters and sold and paid for within the Continental United States and not subject to return.

    (b)   A sum equal to one-half (1/2) of the above sum for ninety (90%) percent of all records manufactured from said Masters and sold outside of the Continental United States. Said sum shall be payable only thirty (30) day s after Purchaser has received such sums in the United States in United States currency.

    (c)   For records sold by way of "club" plans as distinguished from regular retail store sales, Seller shall receive a sum equal to one-half (1/2) the applicable royalty set forth in sub-paragraphs (a) or (b) hereof.

    (d)   In the event Masters hereunder are coupled or released together with Masters not subject to the terms hereof on one recording, Seller will receive that proportion of the royalties payable to it hereinabove as the number of Masters hereunder embodied on such recording bears to the total number of Masters embodied thereon.

* Courtesy of Chas. V. Passantino, New York 10036.

(e)   Retail list price is hereby defined as being the actual retail selling price in the country of manufacture or sale, at Purchaser's option, less taxes, duties and costs of packaging. Monies shall not be payable to Seller for any records given away or sold at less than Purchaser's actual costs therefor.

(f)   The sums above payable are intended to include all monies payable to the recording artists whose performances are embodied on said Masters and Seller agrees to pay and to be solely liable for payment of all monies payable or becoming payable to said recording artists.

4.   Payments of all sums to Seller, except those set forth in Paragraph 3 (b) hereof, shall be made quarterly within sixty (60) days following the calendar quarters ending February 28, May 31, August 31 and November 30 and shall be accompanied by a statement setting forth the computation of such sums. Unless Seller objects, in writing, to any such statement or payment within ninety (90) days after receipt thereof, said statement or payment shall be deemed finally binding upon and accepted by Seller.

5.   (a)   Seller agrees that for a period of five (5) consecutive years from the date of this agreement it will not record or produce nor will it permit others to record or produce phonograph records of a performance by any artist, whose performance is embodied in any master recording which is subject to this agreement of the composition embodied in such master recording, for anyone other than Purchaser.

(b)   Purchaser shall have the option, to be exercised by it in writing within six (6) months from the date hereof, either to secure assignment from Seller of Seller's recording contract with the artists hereunder or to itself enter directly into contract with such artists. If Purchaser exercises either prerogative of said option, Seller will execute all documents necessary to perfect Purchaser's rights in and to the services of such artist. Until the expiration of said six (6) months period, seller will not permit the artist to make any additional recordings nor will it release nor permit to be released any further recordings by the artist which were made prior to the date hereof. Upon exercise of said option, Seller will deliver to Purchaser a sample of any and all master recordings made by the artist and under Seller's control aside from the Masters herein purchased. Said master recordings shall be deemed sold to Purchaser pursuant to all the terms and conditions hereof (with the exception of paragraph _____ of the Rider hereto annexed). Seller agrees to furnish Purchaser with an executed copy of Seller's present agreement with artist upon the execution hereof.

6.   For the purposes hereof, "phonograph record", "record", and "master" are defined as meaning any device of any kind or nature, whether now or hereafter known, for the reproduction of sound.

7.   (a)   This agreement shall be binding upon both Seller and Purchaser and their respective successors and assigns, and shall be deemed effective upon the date of this letter.

(b)   This agreement shall be construed pursuant to and governed by the laws of the State of New York and is the entire agreement between the parties, and cannot be modified except in a writing signed by both parties hereto. Invalidity or unenforceability of any part of this agreement shall not affect the validity and enforceability of the balance hereof.

Very truly yours,

_____

BY _____

Accepted and Agreed to

_____

BY _____

Submitting your master to the record company. You must determine to which record companies you will submit your master. Your decision will probably be influenced by where you live, as you will want to submit it to companies in your vicinity so you may audition your masters personally.

Call up the company and make an appointment with the A & R director. Persist in getting a personal audition, but, if circumstances dictate your mailing the tape or acetate in, be sure to enclose a letter of introduction, all pertinent information as described above, and a self-addressed stamped envelope for return of your material if rejected. If it is wanted, you will be called for an interview. If they offer you a production contract, hire a music attorney to review it before signing. (A discussion on types of production deals appears in chapter 8.)

Starting Your Own Record Company

If you cannot interest a record company to purchase your master and are still convinced you have a winner on hand, you can take the last alternative: put it out yourself by forming your own record company. This consists of the following:

Copyright administration. You must properly file certain copyright registration forms. (A discussion regarding these forms appears in chapter 4.)

Collecting performance royalties. In order for your song to earn substantial income from performances through radio, television, and other users of music, besides affiliating yourself with a performing rights organization, the copyright should be assigned to a publishing company with the capacity to undertake major exploitation of the work. You can either start your own publishing company, as described in chapter 14, or interest another publisher to control and exploit your copyright.

Name the record company. You must select a name for your company. To make sure the name you select does not conflict with an existing company's name, check any of the sources in chapter 6 that contain lists of record companies or check with the various mechanical rights organizations, AF of M, or the *Billboard International Buyer's Guide,* which provides such information.

Register the company. Local business laws may require you to register your company as a business enterprise with the city clerk or city hall. They may only require you to deposit some business stationery with them; however it is highly recommended you consult an attorney when doing this.

Have records pressed. When your master is completed to your satisfaction, you are ready to have records pressed from it. If you know of no companies that press records, check the sources in chapter 6 that contain lists of companies that do or your classified telephone directory. Have no more than a few thousand records pressed initially.

Printed information on the record's label. There is certain information that should be included on the label that adheres to each pressed record's face. This is:

1. The name of the song, artist, writer(s), publishing company and its affiliated performing rights organization, and the length of the song.
2. The record company's name and address—required by the statutory business laws of many states.
3. Naming the country of manufacture—for singles this usually appears as: "Made in U.S.A.," and for albums, as: "Printed in U.S.A."
4. Printing the proper copyright notice for sound recordings. Example: ℗ 1977 John Doe Records, Inc.
5. Printing proper trademark information—for companies with registered trademarks, the words "Registered in U.S. Patent Office," "Reg. U.S. Pat. Off.," or ® must appear on the record label for singles, and record labels and covers for albums. If the company is pending registration, it should substitute the word "Trademark" or "TM" accordingly until registration has been effected.
6. It is not mandatory, but you may wish to have a company logo designed and printed on the record label. The company that presses your records could assist you in finding an artist to create this.

Information on album covers (liner notes) may be protected by printing the copyright notice. This notice consists of the symbol for copyright, © (or the word itself); the year of publication; and the name of the copyright proprietor. This might, for example, look like: © 1977 John Doe Records, Inc. To copyright an album cover with liner notes, register Form KK * with the Copyright Office.

Record promotion. People won't buy a record unless they hear it first. Therefore, you will have to see to it that the song is played on the radio. You can hire a promotion man or team to get airplay for your record as well as contact program directors yourself.

Record distribution. You will contract a distributor to get copies of your record into the stores. This is usually done on a local basis at first. The distributor will either work on a percentage basis or will pay only on records sold. If a certain amount of units (records) is sold, then a major label might be interested in picking up your record (often referred to as a ''hot master'') and handling the promotion and distribution of the record on a national basis themselves. Many hits have started out this way.

If you become successful and knowledgeable from your venture, you might consider keeping your record company active and make a distribution deal with a major label to handle all your products. This is difficult to obtain, but if you have proven you can create and sell a commercial product, you will undoubtedly find a company willing to take a chance on you.

The preceding, of course, is an oversimplified method for a procedure that is complex and risky. If you decide to release your record through your own record company, consult a music attorney and, if possible, an experienced record company employee for advice and guidance.

---

* Subject to change by the Copyright Office effective January 1, 1978.

16: Jingles

A JINGLE IS a short, catchy phrase of music usually accompanied by lyrics whose purpose is to advertise or promote a product or service.

Types of Jingles

The material used for jingles is one of two types. The jingle can be original music and lyrics written specially to convey the commercial message or be a performance of a musical work, usually a familiar tune, originally written for other purposes and adapted into a jingle by use of specially written lyrics used to present the advertising message.

The Jingle as an Effective Advertising Device

Jingles can have a large impact on the sale of a product, and advertisers fully realize this. The use of a musical commercial has been found to be one of the most effective forms of advertising. Our own experience with the jingle blitz by the commercial media can be used as a proving ground for this.

Let's take, for example, some jingles that have saturated the media. Chances are we cannot recite the particular phrase that has been coined for the jingle without associating in our minds the accompanying melody. Try this little experiment with the following three phrases.

"You deserve a break today at McDonald's"
"I'd like to buy the world a Coke"
"N-E-S-T-L-E-S, Nestles make the very best . . . chocolate"

Difficult, isn't it? The melodies have become part of the natural terrain of our subconscious. Their ability to remain with us proves the effectiveness and potential of a jingle.

Breaking In

Breaking in to the competitive market of writing jingles is difficult, as is any area of songwriting. Most of the jingles written for well-known products are commissioned by the advertising agency hired by the manufacturer of the product. Advertising agencies either have the creative personnel to write jingles themselves or farm the job out to music houses equipped with their own staff of composers and writers who also arrange and produce the jingle.

Due to the existing situation, a more practical way for a songwriter wishing entry into the jingle field might be for him to start writing jingles for local entrepreneurs. There are several local merchants, such as car dealers or small food chains that might be receptive to your submitting a sample jingle to advertise their products or services. One jingle that had begun on a local level and later rose to national prominence as a pop song and has become a standard among popular songs is Paul Williams' "We've Only Just Begun," originally written for the Crocker Bank in San Francisco. (For writers wishing to try their skill at writing jingles for nationally known products, a list of many of these appear in Appendix D along with the advertising agency's name and address in charge of its account.)

Writing Jingles

To write a jingle, simply coin a short phrase, one that is easy to remember and includes the particular product's or service's name you are writing for and set a simple, catchy melody to it.

Writing jingles for use in film is a specialized field within a field. Certain rhythmic patterns and notes have to coincide with filmed action or within exact frames so many spots must contain time changes in the music. As in setting music for motion pictures (see chapter 17), a click track is often used. Writing for this particular medium requires special training and experience.

Income

When a well-known song is used as a jingle or in association with an advertiser's product, a license fee is negotiated with the copyright owner. License fees in these cases are determined by the prestige of the song being negotiated, the extent of the territories to be licensed (i.e. local, regional, national, or international), and the length of time in which the jingle may be used. The advertiser will negotiate for an exclusive license to the song so other companies cannot use it to advertise their product. License fees for use of "standard" songs have ranged from hundreds to tens of thousands of dollars.

For original music written specially for a product, the usual contractual agreement is for a flat fee to be paid by the advertising agency (on behalf of its client) to the composer. In these cases, the writer usually licenses the work directly to the ad agency. The writer should, however, try to retain the right to collect the performance royalties distributed by a performing rights organization. The writer should also attempt to retain the publishing rights to his tune. Despite the fact that a jingle receives airplay, it is not considered a true song unless its lyric is rewritten in a manner which will make it relate to a more universal experience. Many advertising agencies own music publishing companies to collect the additional revenue a jingle can generate if this happens. Many writers, however, sell the rights to their original melody to the advertising agency for use as a jingle, while retaining the right to publish it as a song.

Performance Royalties

The usual agreement between the jingle writer and advertising agency does not permit the writer to receive performance royalties. These contracts call for the writer to license the work directly to the agency.

To earn performance royalties, the writer must have a contract with the agency which specifically reserves the performing rights to the writer. In these cases, the writer is eligible to receive performance royalties from ASCAP or SESAC if he is a member of either organization. As a member of ASCAP, the writer receives 1 percent of an ASCAP "use" credit for all performances of the jingle within any one-hour period. For all performances in the second hour, the writer receives .1 percent of an ASCAP "use" credit. The number of credits that make up a "use" credit depend upon the strata in which the work is performed (i.e., local radio, network television, etc.). SESAC makes payments for performances of jingles based upon the media in which the work is performed and whether the jingle is performed on a national, regional, or local basis.

BMI does not make payment to writers or publishers for performances of a jingle.

Payment to Performers of Jingles

Jingle singers and musicians get paid a session fee and collect residuals based on the amount of airplay the jingle is given. Minimum rates of payment to singers are determined by AFTRA (American Federation of Television and Radio Artists) and SAG (Screen Actors Guild). Fees for radio jingles normally come under AFTRA jurisdiction and those for television under SAG jurisdiction. Minimum rates of payment to musicians are determined by the AF of M (American Federation of Musicians).

Airplay

Whereas airplay for records is determined by a song's appeal and promotional efforts on behalf of the record company, airplay for jingles is bought by the advertiser.

17: Writing Music for Motion Pictures

THERE ARE TWO SIDES to the life of today's film composer—the glamorous side and the nervous-breakdown side. Since we all like the finer things in life, let's first look at the glamorous side.

The top-flight movie composer earns a yearly six-figure income, has a sprawling Beverly Hills mansion, dresses in the most expensive clothes, eats at the best restaurants, and drives the flashiest cars. On the other hand (the cerebral ulcer side), he has eighteen-hour work days; has to write to please studio executives, sometimes yielding artistic compromise; and has ridiculously short deadlines within which to do this.

Once a composer has broken into this specialized field, the secret to *perpetuating* his career is speed (being able to knock off a score within a minimum of time) and composing music that pleases the Hollywood Establishment—the producer, director, and studio chiefs. Let's examine this in more detail.

Work Schedule

Film composers work long days because they have deadlines. There is no time for inspiration or, many times, the artistic perfection afforded the concert composer. Complete scores are often required within three to four weeks. The composer will develop a close working relationship with the producer or director from the outset of the movie in an effort to musically underscore the development of the theme, of the characters, and of various passages.

Technique

A common technique for scoring is this: the composer will initially view the film several times alone and then "spot" it with the producer or director to determine where music should start and stop. The composer then watches the film on a moviola. A moviola is a projection machine that reduces the film to a four-inch viewing screen that can be started, stopped, or reversed at will. Separate soundtracks for the voices are heard through small speakers. With a stopwatch and click track, the composer determines how much music can be inserted in a "spot." A click track is a perforated soundtrack producing click sounds that enable the operator to hear a predetermined beat in synchronization with the movie. The composer will write music to be placed within predetermined intervals and will then orchestrate it into a full score or he will sketch the melody lines and have someone else orchestrate it.

Training

The technical training needed to score motion pictures requires a considerable amount of education and experience. Such courses as orchestration, film scoring, conducting, counterpoint, harmony, ear training, and dictation are invaluable if not prerequisite. Then, much practical experience is necessary in working with tools integral to scoring films such as moviolas, click tracks, time sheets, footage charts, and stopwatches.

Songwriters who compose songs that sound like motion picture themes have little chance in placing it in such a medium. A director of BMI says: "There is virtually no hope for the individual who just writes themes that would be appropriate or could be developed for motion pictures. He must be able to score the picture he writes the theme for.'' Regardless of how good one's theme is, most film composers will not score a picture for which somebody else (especially an unknown) has written the theme.

Breaking In

After you have acquired the necessary skills to score a film, it is still difficult to break in. Since most of the domestic film productions are done in Hollywood, you would probably have to live there and immerse yourself full time in pursuing this career.

One way to break in is to ''apprentice'' with an established film composer. Such composers often have an excessive amount of work to be finished within narrow deadlines, so they may farm out some of their work; perhaps they will sketch a score and have you orchestrate it, or they might be generous enough to offer you one of their complete assignments. If you do a good job, you will get more and more work to do, build up a good reputation, and create a demand for yourself. Or, if you can find an agent who believes in your ability, he, too, could help you get your foot in the door.

Types of Contracts for Original Compositions in Motion Pictures

The services of a composer or lyricist might be engaged by a motion picture producer in any of the following ways:

''Employee-for-hire'' basis. When original music and songs are desired for a motion picture, the writers might be hired on what is referred to as an ''employee-for-hire'' basis. In such a contract, the writers are deemed employees of the producer or motion picture company and all rights to ownership of the copyright become the property of the producer or motion picture company. Copyright registration, renewal, and extension is filed by these employers. As Title 17, *U.S. Code,* Section 201(b) * states: ''In the case of a work made for hire, the employer or other person for whom the work was prepared is considered the author for purposes of this title, and, unless the par-

---

* As stated by the copyright law effective January 1, 1978.

ties have expressly agreed otherwise in a written instrument signed by them, owns all of the rights comprised in the copyright.''

Part ownership of copyright. Composers and lyricists sometimes receive an ownership to their copyright in exchange for their accepting a fee lower than they would normally receive for their services. Under such an agreement, the writer is not considered an ''employee-for-hire'' and is the proprietor for a portion of the copyright mutually agreed upon with the other copyright owner.

Full ownership of copyright. Some more prominent film composers in addition to receiving a fee to compose a score, retain the rights for all uses of the copyright and grant to the motion picture company or producer a license to use the copyright in the particular picture for which it was written.

Required Rights for Use of Music in Motion Pictures

A motion picture producer must obtain two basic rights to use music and lyrics in his film. These are synchronization rights and performing rights. In cases where original music is created for the film, he usually becomes the proprietor of these rights by virtue of his ''employer'' status. In cases where music was created for other purposes, he must obtain a synchronization and performance license from the copyright owner or the mechanical rights organization administering the owner's copyright for such licensing purposes.

Sources of Income

Original compositions. Under an ''employee-for-hire'' contract, composers and lyricists generally grant to the producer or motion picture company all rights in the copyright with the specification of royalties to be paid to the composer and lyricist from their writers' share of the income. This income might result from performances of the work, the issuance of synchronization and mechanical licenses, and sales of sheet music and other printed editions containing the copyright.

Compositions created for other purposes. In this circumstance, the motion picture producer will negotiate with the copyright proprietor for a synchronization and performance license. Factors used in determining this license fee include the importance of the song to the movie, the number of times the song occurs in the film, and how long it runs for each use. The producer will also seek in this license permission to exhibit the film without restriction. The publisher, or mechanical rights organization acting on its behalf, however, may wish to limit exploitation to certain media and be entitled to receive additional fees for further exploitation. He may, for instance, opt for more money for exhibition of the film on pay television or cable TV. The time period for which the license is granted is also another factor used in determining the license fee.

In the United States, copyright owners do not receive from the performing rights organizations royalties for the performance of their works in theatrical motion pictures. Such right is licensed directly to the producer, rather than the exhibitor of the film. For European exhibitions of films containing their copyrights, copyright owners receive royalties from performing rights organizations. European theaters pay a percentage of their net box-office receipts to the performing rights society in their country which in turn pays the copyright owners through their domestic performing rights organization.

Television. When a copyright owner's song is performed on United States television, he receives a synchronization fee, which is paid for the right to use the work in synchronization (timed relation) to the film. In addition, performance income is derived from the broadcast of the composition, which is monitored and logged by the performing rights organizations.

Soundtracks. When the composer is also the conductor of a score released as a commercial soundtrack, he often obtains from the producer or motion picture company an agreement which provides for a recording artist royalty with respect to any sales of commercial phonograph records made from the film's soundtrack. This royalty usually ranges from 2.5 to 5 percent of all records sold in the United States based upon the retail list price. Such contract agreements customarily provide for a smaller royalty to the composer-conductor with regard to foreign or record club sales of the soundtrack.

18: Writing Music for the Theater

THE MUSICAL IS yet another medium which songwriters strive to break into. It is an extremely competitive market because only a relatively small number of shows are produced and an even fewer number are successful. Musicals are expensive to produce and many people can hardly afford the high cost of a ticket. People will, however, pay to see a play if it has a good story and memorable music. There is always the need for quality musicals; so as difficult as it is to break into this area, the challenge, as history shows, can be met by the unknown but talented songwriter.

Show Music

The music played in today's stage show ranges in style from that which is traditionally found in musicals to that which we find at the top of today's charts. It is very common now for artists to record show tunes and have great commercial success with them. *Hair, Jesus Christ Superstar, Godspell,* and *The Wiz* are among the many contemporary musicals from which songs transcended the Broadway theaters at which they were performed into the homes of people around the world via the top 40. Producers and "angels" (financial backers of a play) express greater interest in musicals that have one or more potential hits because of the free publicity a hit song will generate for the show.

Writing the Musical Stage Show

Writers of popular songs are often asked how they got their ideas for writing songs and which comes first—the music or the lyrics? Songwriters have their own methods of writing and the answer to this depends upon the individual songwriter's creativity and technique. In the writing of musical shows, however, there is almost always a precedent to the writing of songs—the play. Plays may be adaptations from existing books or be the original work of a playwright. It is the rare exception for a play to be written from one's musical score and lyrics.

If you are interested in writing songs for a show, you should find a playwright with an available and potential script for a musical. It is possible that your creative endowments extend to this area also, but you should not seek this extra capacity if it will mean sacrificing any quality in your music-writing efforts. Write or choose a script to your liking, but be sure it has the elements essential for a successful play— these include a good plot, a subplot, and character development.

Also obvious, but often overlooked, is the fact that many plays don't translate themselves into musical adaptation. Be sure in your mind that the play you are writing music for is appropriate for production as a musical.

When writing songs for the play, be sure they are an integral part of the story. This means the titles, lyrics, and music must illustrate a particular scene, theme, or character. The lyric must complement the music, the music the plot, and each in reverse. Only when all three reach their highest potential is the show ready to begin.

Getting the Show on the Road

One of the best ways to enter this specialized field is by having your musical showcased. There are numerous not-so-amateurish theater companies in local areas that are constantly performing. College theater groups, repertory companies, theater guilds, YMCA groups, civic groups, church and synagogue clubs, and musical workshops are some of the many available groups that actively perform shows.

Once you have an original script and songs, you can contact these people. Convince them your show has qualities that will be loved by their audiences and you will have your play performed. Once it is, generate as much local publicity for it as possible. Then interest music publishers and show producers by inviting them to watch a performance of the show.

If you cannot get a group to perform your show, then submit your script and songs to a producer or publisher anyway. At this point, you are back to marketing and your method of generating interest in your work will be the same as discussed earlier. Be sure to contact those producers and publishers listed on the back of the album covers from popular shows.

The Broadway Musical

Having a show open on Broadway is almost like having a song enter the Top 40. You have reached the most important commercial market and are now in contention for a big hit or smash. The only difference is that with a successful show you stand to earn a lot more money.

The Dramatists Guild, which represents composers and lyricists whose shows are running on Broadway, provides beneficial contract terms for the creators. Such terms call for the writers (composer, lyricist, and book author) to collectively receive a minimum royalty of 6 percent of the theater's gross weekly box-office receipts which is usually divided equally among them. Other contract terms provide for participation by the creators in "subsidiary" rights. This means the writers will receive a fair share of the license fees and royalties from motion pictures, television rights, touring company and amateur productions, and other uses of the play which fall into this category. Normally, the writers of a Broadway show do not grant to the producer the music publishing rights to their score.

Income from original cast albums is another large source of revenue for composers and lyricists. With the increase in compulsory license fees to take effect January 1, 1978, it is anticipated that the negotiated royalties to the copyright owners (composer, lyricist, and book author) will increase per original cast album sold. That is, for an original cast album of twelve songs which is the first recording released of the show's music, the royalty to the copyright owners will increase from a minimum of 24 cents to 33 cents per album sold. Composers and lyricists have been known to earn several thousands of dollars per week while their musicals were running on Broadway.

BMI Theater Workshop

Each year the BMI offices in New York City and Beverly Hills, California, sponsor the BMI Musical Theater Workshop. In an effort to stimulate new talent for the theater, composers and lyricists who are members of the workshop are given assignments in writing musical shows. At the end of the workshop there is a public presentation of selected original material. Writers do not have to be BMI-affiliated to be accepted into this program. Membership is determined by audition and interview.

19: The Song Shark

A SONG SHARK is the individual or company that deals unethically with songwriters by charging them a fee for certain services which the legitimate music publisher expends as a normal cost of business in the exploitation of new songs.

Song sharks fulfill only the mechanics of their promises—whether it be printing a song, setting music to a lyric, or making a recording of the writer's tune. It is their unwillingness and insufficient efforts to make good on their assurances of success that warrants the songwriter to avoid them. No legitimate music publisher or record company will ever charge a fee for the services song sharks sell.

Methods of Operation

Song sharks lure the amateur, uneducated, or discouraged songwriter with advertisements readily found in popular magazines. Captions like "poems wanted for songs and records," or "get into big money career writing songs" immediately attract the aspiring songwriter's attention. Without asking for money in the advertisement, the song sharks ask that material be sent in for "examination" to see if the writer "qualifies" for their services. Songwriters soon find out it's not the quality of their material that makes them qualify, but rather their desire to part with their money.

After sending in his material, the songwriter will get an immediate response proclaiming its potential. The song shark then indicates the next step the writer should take, which, of course, requires the accompaniment of money. This is usually the first in a chain of steps the song shark uses to hook the songwriter, for after his initial investment, the songwriter is called upon to send in more money to take the next step in making his song a "success." The songwriter is easily hooked after his initial investment, as he doesn't want to lose what he's already put it.

Some of the techniques song sharks use to obtain money from the songwriter are:

1. *Payment for "publication" and "plugging."* For a certain sum of money, the song shark says he will print professional copies of the writer's song and distribute them to important people in the music business. Copies of the music are never made available for public purchase. In reality, the songwriter gets a neat, printed copy of his song with his name on it, but finds all attempts, if any, made by the company to make his song a success are fruitless.

2. *Payment for setting a melody to a writer's song poem or lyric.* After indicating the potential a writer's song poem or lyric has, song sharks press to set a melody to it for a fee. Of course, their melodies have no commercial potential, otherwise they would write their own lyric or obtain one from professionals. Most of the melodies they set to the different lyrics sent in are similar to each other. That is so that when they solicit the writer for the next step, to make a demo of his song, they can do it at a cost he can afford. Song sharks have basic music tracks recorded on tape that only require a vocal overdub to make a complete demo. The song shark will fashion the writer's lyric to fit the pattern of the music on the track and overdub it with the lyric and one of his old melodies or a variation of it. In this way he can make demos, cheaply but quickly, and devote more time to the solicitation of orders.

3. *Payment for setting a lyric to a melody.* The song shark has no difficulty in creating a lyric to fit a writer's melody. He has no concern regarding the potential of the lyric he sets to it nor the quality of the writer's melody. His only concern is that he is paid for what he does.

4. *Payment for record production and release.* Song sharks advertise that they will professionally record a writer's song, press cop-

ies of it, and release it to broadcasting stations—all for a fee. This is contrary to the operations of a legitimate record company.

A writer whose song has been continually rejected might feel that by this procedure the public will finally be able to hear his song and judge for themselves his talent. What actually happens is that the writer gets a poorly produced recording of his song that has no commercial potential. The song also receives little or no promotion to radio stations; thus, the writer has paid for a record that will not even return the investment he made to create it. But the song shark will seek even more money from the songwriter when he tells him what potential the record has and asks for more money to have a large quantity of records pressed.

In conclusion, songwriters should be aware of the following: Legitimate music publishing companies never charge a fee to publish a song; a legitimate collaborator will not charge a fee for creating his part (he receives a percentage of the writer's share of the copyright); legitimate record companies do not charge a writer in advance of sales the costs to make the record, nor ever charge for record pressing expenses; and no individual or company can ever "guarantee" you a hit record.

When in Doubt—Check Them Out

A songwriter who is unsure of the legitimacy of a soliciting music publisher may contact any of the performing rights organizations, AGAC, if a member, the Better Business Bureau, or the consumer frauds agency in the state in which the company in question is doing business, for an opinion as to whether he is dealing with a song shark.

20: Songwriting Workshops

Objectives of the Songwriting Workshop

The purpose of a songwriting workshop is to bring songwriters together for an exchange of advice and ideas that will help further their abilities and careers.

The workshop should devote itself to enabling the songwriter to make the most out of his ability and to educate himself in those music business matters that will help further his career as a songwriter. To achieve these objectives, the workshop will have to be run in such a way that it includes training in music and lyric writing, instruction in music business procedures, showcasing and evaluation of songs, and a time period allotted to a free exchange of ideas and working methods.

Writers must not be afraid to make mistakes at the workshop meetings and correct them by trial and error. The route to a successful workshop is a steady and constant stream of creative ideas emanating from a sincere desire on behalf of the songwriter to improve his talents by correcting his flaws.

Collaboration

One of the important benefits of a songwriting workshop is the large selection of songwriters from which one may choose a collaborator. Those whose talents reside in either music or lyric writing can choose a collaborator who is prolific in the area they are not.

If you and your collaborator are members of the same workshop, chances are you both live within close proximity to each other. This is beneficial as you both can devote more personal attention to each other's work. If you and your collaborator are unable to arrange personal meetings, the lyric writer may submit a copy of his work to the composer. In cases where the music is written first, the composer can play his melody on a cassette and submit that to the lyricist. In each case, the use of cassette tape to hear the step-by-step results is found to be of great value as it is easy to operate and convenient to use.

If you are unable to find a collaborator from your workshop, advertisements in the local press or trade journals may produce a suitable partner for you.

Showcasing

Showcasing of original songs is one of the most, if not the most, important aspects of a songwriting workshop. It provides the opportunity for songwriters to receive an honest appraisal of their writing efforts, which may result in their correcting some unrecognized mistakes and improving their songs and ability. Writers should be open-minded so that if criticism is warranted they will rework the particular weak spots.

Just as you would want an honest evaluation of your material, you should be constructive in your evaluation of others. You might be surprised by how much you can learn from analyzing and evaluating new songs by other writers. It is recommended that all songs showcased during the workshop be copyrighted.

Starting a Songwriting Workshop

Many communities presently have songwriting workshops. You can find out if there is one in yours by contacting local music stores or schools. If you are unable to find one, however, you may wish to start your own.

To start a songwriting workshop you will first have to find other songwriters. This will require a little leg work, but in the end it will be worth your while. You can generate publicity by posting signs in music and record shops, libraries, notifying local schools, musicians, and teachers and by running advertisements in the local press. Wait and see the results. You will be surprised by the amount of people who share your interest.

When you feel you have enough people interested in joining, you are ready to get the ball rolling. You will need a meeting place, but this problem can be easily solved. Meetings can be held on a rotating basis at each member's house or at a designated meeting place. Perhaps your public library or some local group will donate a room or charge a nominal fee for this. If you decide to charge dues, make it within the means of every member.

It may be to your advantage to contact ASCAP, BMI, or SESAC when getting started. They often sponsor workshops in large cities and their expertise might be beneficial for your workshop. They might suggest ways to improve your organization and even recommend an experienced songwriter in your vicinity to aid you. It is, of course, to the advantage of every member to have a successful songwriter who faced the same problems all amateur songwriters face available at each meeting to guide and instruct workshop members. If such a person is not available, then it will be up to each member of the workshop to prepare himself sufficiently in a topic of his own choosing whereby other members may gain from his knowledge.

The group might be fortunate to get someone who works in the music industry to come to a meeting and lecture. Write or call such personnel in your area. A knowledgeable and experienced music business employee can make invaluable contributions to the workshop.

Workshop Incentives

Whatever you do, always make the workshop work to the group's best advantage. There are incentives you might devise to further the careers of workshop members. For instance, you might contact a local radio station to sponsor a songwriting contest where the winner will be interviewed on the air and have his song broadcast, or interest a local merchant in sponsoring a jingle contest to help promote his product. Your creativity in developing incentives might work to your very own advantage.

Sample Songwriting Workshop Program

Songwriting workshops may be long-term or have a predetermined syllabus with goals to be accomplished within a designated time period. The following pages contain a sample workshop program of the latter's nature that was constructed from the contents of this book, after which you may wish to model yours. An eight-meeting series was devised for which a syllabus lists the topics to be discussed and other goals to be accomplished. Following the syllabus are certain lists, questionnaires, and forms pertinent to the establishment and growth of a successful workshop.

Sample Syllabus

Session I: *Introduction and Registration*
   a) introduction to the workshop
   b) meet other songwriters
   c) so you've written a song—what's next?
   d) sign up and showcase of songs
   e) question and answer session/discussion period
Session II: *Writing Commercial Song Lyrics*
   a) the title
   b) elements of the commercial lyric
   c) setting a lyric to music
   d) how to find and develop lyrical ideas
   e) assignment in lyric writing
   f) showcase
   g) question and answer/discussion period
Session III: *Writing Music*
   a) writing melody (structure, range and key)
   b) rhythm

c) harmony
d) setting music to a lyric
e) the hook
f) how to find and develop musical ideas
g) assignment in writing music
h) showcase
i) question and answer/discussion period

Session IV: *Music Business for the Songwriter—Part I*
a) writing lead sheets
b) demos
c) copyrights
d) how to get your songs commercially recorded
e) how to get the most out of trade magazines
f) showcase
g) question and answer/discussion period

Session V: *Music Business for the Songwriter—Part II*
a) the music publisher
b) the record producer
c) A & R directors
d) showcase
e) question and answer/discussion period

Session VI: *Music Business for the Songwriter—Part III*
a) performing rights organizations
b) mechanical rights organizations
c) how to publish your own music
d) showcase
e) question and answer/discussion period

Session VII: *Music Business for the Songwriter—Part IV*
a) writing music for motion pictures
b) writing music for the theater
c) jingles
d) assignment in jingle writing
e) showcase
f) question and answer/discussion period

Session VIII: *Music Business for the Songwriter—Part V*
a) the singer-songwriter
b) making your own masters and selling them
c) songwriter contracts
d) analyzing the commercial market

e) showcase

f) question and answer/discussion period

Songwriting Workshop Format

1. Weekly, two-hour meetings:
   a) 1 hour instruction period
   b) ½ hour showcase of new songs
   c) ½ hour question and answer session/discussion period (ideas and suggestions)
2. collaboration service
3. question and answer service
4. evaluation of songs and referrals—where/who to take them to
5. newsletter
6. latest information of use in the music world
7. demo service—if enough people want professional demos made, we can produce quality demos at a discount
8. guest speakers—professionals from the music business
9. music and lyric writing exercises, and lists of important publishers and record companies to be distributed to members
10. workshop "library"—songwriter books, trade magazines, and other materials available for use by members
11. songwriting contest—with the winner to be interviewed and have his song played on a local radio station.

Songwriter's Questionnaire

Name

Address

Telephone   Age

Present Occupation

Educational Background

Affiliation   ASCAP   BMI   SESAC

  None   Other_____

Have you copyrighted any of your songs?

Have you had any songs under contract to a music publisher?

Have you had any songs commercially recorded?

How many songs have you written?

How long have you been writing songs?

Can you write a lead sheet?

Can you write your own arrangements?

Have you had any experience in theater, film, commercials, or performing groups? If yes, please explain.

Do you play any musical instruments? Which ones?

Do you sing?

Do you own a cassette recorder, reel-to-reel tape recorder, or stereo?

Who are your three favorite songwriters?

Which are your three favorite songs?

How do you think these workshop sessions might be of most value to you?

Who would you like to have as guest speakers?

Do you have any "contacts"?

Additional remarks/credits:

Songwriter Showcase Information

How can you best show your songs?
1. Tape or acetate demo
2. Live performance
3. Play on an instrument
4. Lead sheet only

Collaboration Information

1. Do you wish a collaborator?
2. Do you write music _____ lyrics _____ both _____
3. In which specialty do you prefer a collaborator, words or music?
4. How much time do you have to devote to working with a collaborator?
5. Do you have any preferences? (age, etc.)
6. Additional remarks:

_____

Registration Form

_____ fee payable to Songwriters' Workshop

Name _____

Street address _____ Paid _____

City _____ State _____ Zip _____

21: Analyzing the Commercial Market

THE COMMERCIAL MUSIC MARKET consists of three major areas: pop, rhythm and blues, and country and western. There are spinoff markets from these such as easy listening and gospel.

Crossovers

When a song receives airplay in more than one market, it is said to be a "crossover." Some country and western songs, for instance, become hits on pop stations and vice versa. "Fairytale" by The Pointer Sisters was a soul hit in 1974 that reached the top of the charts in the country and western market, one of the few times a crossover has occurred between an R & B and country and western record.

Some Sources for Analyzing the Commercial Market

The radio is the best source for analyzing a commercial market. Listen to songs and try to determine why each song has achieved success to one degree or another. Determine why somebody would go out and buy that particular record. Be open-minded!

The charts in the trades are another great source to analyze the commercial music market. The charts list the titles, artists, producers, publishers, and record companies of the most successful records each week.

Sheet music permits you to analyze a song visually and by playing it if you can read music. Melodies are written out in musical notation with the corresponding chords and lyics.

Buying a record and playing it over and over again will also help you to analyze its success. Repeated listenings will permit you to closer analyze the arrangement, production, and artist's performance.

Contributing Factors to a Hit Record

There are several factors that contribute to a record's success. A hit record is always the result of the efforts of many people. No one person is ever singularly responsible for the sales a record achieves. The marriage of the following factors helps in making a record successful:

1. song
2. artist
3. arrangement
4. production
5. time of release
6. place of release
7. promotion
8. distribution.

In your analysis of records, you will only be able to make an evaluation of the song, artist, arrangement, and production. The others are variables that depend upon the strength and experience of the record company issuing the record.

When writing songs, you should try to write the type that you regularly listen to on the radio and like most. Always be aware, most importantly, of what's commercial. Public taste is not always possible to predict; that is why you may often hear songs played on the radio which you dislike.

Compare the songs you write to the ones you analyze. After you go through all the studies previously discussed and are still convinced your song has it "in the grooves," pursue it. As they might say in the music business, you have a "monster!"

Appendix A: The Songwriter's Glossary

AABA. A commonly used song pattern consisting of two verses, a bridge, and a verse, where the verses are musically the same.

Acetate dub. An individually cut record (as opposed to pressed records).

Administration. The supervision of all financial, copyright, and contractual aspects of either an entire catalog or a particular song.

Advance. Money paid before the recording or release of a song, to be deducted against future royalties of that song.

AF of M. American Federation of Musicians; unions for musicians, arrangers, copyists, contractors, and orchestrators.

AFTRA. American Federation of Television and Radio Artists; union for singers, actors, announcers, narrators, and sound effects artists.

AGAC. American Guild of Authors and Composers; a songwriter's protective association.

Angel. The financial backer of a play.

A & R director. Artists and repertoire; record company employee in charge of selecting new artists, songs, and masters.

Arrangement. The adaptation of a composition for performance by other instruments and voices than originally intended.

Artist. Individual or group under recording contract.

ASCAP. American Society of Composers, Authors and Publishers; a performing rights organization.

Assignment. The transfer of rights to a song or catalog from one copyright proprietor to another.

BMI. Broadcast Music, Inc.; a performing rights organization.

Booking agent. One who finds employment for artists from buyers of talent.

Bootlegging. The unauthorized recording and selling of a performance of the song.

Bridge. The section of music that links verses together in a song.

Bullet. Designation of a record listed on the charts, referring to increased record sales.

Catalog. All the songs owned by a music publisher considered as one collection.

Charts. Lists published in the trade magazines of the best-selling records. There are separate charts for pop, soul, and country and western songs; musical arrangements.

Chord. Three or more notes sounded simultaneously that imply a harmonic function.

Chorus. A section of the song that repeats itself at certain intervals.

Clearance. The right of a radio station to play a song.

Clearance agency. See **Performing rights organization.**

Click track. A perforated soundtrack that produces click sounds that enables one to hear a predetermined beat in synchronization with the movie.

Collaborator. One of two or more partners in the writing of songs.

CMA. Country Music Association; organization devoted to promoting country music.

Commercial. The potential to sell; that which has mass appeal.

Common-law copyright. Natural protection of a song based on common laws of the various states. To be superseded by a single national system effective January 1, 1978.

Composer. One who writes the music to a song.

Composition. A musical work; the art of writing music.

Compulsory license (Phonorecords). Statutory mandate given to a copyright owner to permit third parties to make sound recordings of the copyright owner's song after it once has been recorded.

Copyright (n.). The exclusive rights granted to authors and composers for protection of their works; a song or musical composition.

Copyright (v.). To secure protection for a song by filing the proper registration forms with the Copyright Office.

Copyright infringement. Stealing or using somebody else's copyrighted song.

Copyright notice. Notice comprised of three elements:
  1. the symbol of copyright—©, the word "copyright," or the abbreviation "Copr."
  2. the year the song has been registered for copyright or the year of first publication of the work
  3. the copyright owner's name.

Copyright Office. Federal government department, one of whose main purposes is to file and supply information regarding copyrights.

Copyright owner. The owner of any one of the exclusive rights comprised in a copyright.

Copyright Royalty Tribunal. A committee created by Public Law 94-553 to determine adjustments starting January 1, 1978, of royalty rates with respect to compulsory licenses for educational television, cable television, jukeboxes, and sound recordings.

Cover record. Another artist's version of a song already recorded.

Crossover. A song which receives airplay in more than one market.

Cut. To record; a recorded selection.

C & W. Country and western.

Date. A recording session.

Diazo process white-print reproduction. Reproduction of musical manuscripts by use of an onion-skin master.

Demo. A demonstration recording of a song used to show its potential to music industry personnel.

Distributor. Company that exclusively handles the sale of a record company's product to jobbers and retail outlets for a certain territory.

Employee-for-hire. Contractual basis whereby a motion picture producer or company employs a composer or lyricist to create music or songs for a movie with copyright ownership to be retained by the producer or company.

Engineer. Individual who operates studio equipment during the recording of a song.

Folio. A collection of songs offered for sale to the public.

Form E. Copyright registration form for protection of musical works.

Form N. Copyright registration form filed for protection of sound recordings.

Form U. Copyright registration form to be filed by the copyright owner when he has first recorded his song or licensed it for recording on mechanical instruments such as phonograph records.

Gold Album. Certification by the Recording Industry of America that an album has sold half a million units.

Gold Single. Certification by the Recording Industry of America that a single has sold one million units.

Grammy. Music industry awards presented by the National Academy of Recording Arts and Sciences (NARAS).

Groove. Rhythm or tempo that helps create the "feel" of the song.

Harmony. The combination of musical notes to form chords that serve to enhance the melody line; the art of combining notes into chords.

Harry Fox Agency. An organization which represents music publishers in connection with the mechanical reproduction of their copyrights as well as the use of their compositions for motion picture synchronization.

Hit. A record that sells many copies; a description applied to records that achieve top 40 status.

Hook. A phrase or melody line that repeats itself in a song; the "catchy" part to a song.

"Head" arrangement. An arrangement devised spontaneously. No charts are prepared for instrumentalists and vocalists. Instead, they read off lead sheets and an arrangement is made from various experimental stylings devised at the studio.

Ink. To sign a contract.

Jingle. A short phrase of music usually accompanied by lyrics used to convey a commercial message.

LP. A long-playing record played at 33 1/3 revolutions per minute (rpm).

Label. A record company.

Lead sheet. A musical notation of a song's melody along with the chord symbols, words, and other pertinent information.

Leadered tape. Reel-to-reel tape which contains songs separated by white tape for easy access.

License (n.). A legal permit.

License (v.). To authorize by legal permit.

Lick. A brief, improvised musical interpolation.

Logo. An artistic design found on records and album covers that identify the company issuing the product.

Lyrics. The words to a song.

Lyric sheet. A (typed) copy of the lyrics to a song.

Lyricist. The writer of the words to a song.

Manager. One who guides an artist in the development of his career.

Market. Selling place; medium where only one type of record is played (i.e. pop, R & B, C & W, etc.).

Master. A finished recording of the song from which records are pressed and distributed to radio stations and record stores.

Mechanical right. Right granted by U.S. copyright law to a copyright owner to profit from the mechanical reproduction of his song.

Mechanical rights organization. Collection agency for copyright owners of moneys earned from the mechanical reproduction of their songs.

Mechanical royalties. Moneys earned for use of a copyright in mechanical reproductions, most notably records and tapes.

Mix. Blending together the tracks of a multitrack recording.

Modulate. To change from one key to another in a song.

MOR. "Middle of the road"; songs that may be classified as easy listening.

Motif. The shortest significant melody of a song or theme.

Moviola. A projection machine that reduces film to a small viewing screen.

Music publisher. The individual or company who:

1. screen songs and gets them commercially recorded
2. exploits the copyrights
3. protects the copyrights
4. collects income from performance, mechanical, synchronization, and printing rights both in the United States and in foreign countries.

Neutral demo. A demo that doesn't sound like it's for one particular artist, but best represents the song whereby it can be recorded by anybody.

One-stop. Wholesale record dealer that sells the records of several manufacturers to jukebox operators and record stores.

Overdub. The addition of instruments or voices to pre-existing tracks.

Payola. Secret payment to broadcasters to play certain records.

Pen. To compose or write.

Performing right. Right granted by U.S. copyright law which states that one may not publicly perform a copyrighted musical work without the owner's permission.

Performing rights organization. Organization whose purpose is to collect moneys earned from public performances of songs by users of music and to distribute these to the writers and publishers of these songs in a proportion that reflects as accurately as possible the amount of performances of each particular song.

Performance royalties. Moneys earned from use of one's song on radio, television, and other users of music.

Phonorecord. Any device which transmits sound other than that which accompanies a motion picture or other audiovisual work.

Photo-offset reproduction. Reproduction of musical manuscript by printing press.

Pick. A song that has been reviewed by the trades and projected to have success.

Pirating. The unauthorized reproduction and selling of sound recordings (i.e. records and tapes).

Pitch. To audition or sell; the position of a tone in the musical scale.

Platinum Album. Certification by the Recording Industry Association of America that an album has sold one million units.

Platinum Single. Certification by the Recording Industry Association of America that a single has sold two million units.

Plug. Broadcast of a song; to push for a song's performance.

Plugola. Secret payment to broadcasters for free mention of products on the air.

Points. A percentage of money producers and artists earn based on the retail list price of 90 percent of all records sold.

Press. The manufacture of a large quantity of records duplicated from a master for commercial sale.

Professional manager. The person in charge of screening new material for music publishers and of obtaining commercial recordings of songs in his company's catalog.

Producer. The individual who oversees the making of a record from the selection of the song to its completion as a master.

Program director. Radio station employee who determines which songs shall be broadcast.

Publication. The printing and distribution of copies of a work to the public by sale or other transfer of ownership, or by rental, lease, or lending.

Public domain. Unprotected by copyright due to an expired copyright or caused by an invalid copyright notice.

R & B. Rhythm and blues; "soul" music.

Rack jobber. Dealer that supplies records of many manufacturers to certain retail outlets such as drugstores, variety stores, and supermarkets.

Release. The issuing of a record by the record company.

Royalty. Money earned from use of the record or song.

Self-contained artist. An artist who writes and performs his own material.

SESAC. A performing rights, mechanical rights, and synchronization licensing organization.

Session. Meeting during which time musicians and vocalists make a recording.

Sheet music. Printed editions of a single song offered for sale to the public.

Showcase. A presentation of new songs and/or talent.

Single. A small record played at 45 rpms containing two selections, one on each side; record released because of the expectation by the record company that the "A" side would achieve success.

Song plugger. One who auditions songs for performers.

Song shark. One who profits from dealing with songwriters by deceptive methods.

Speculation. The recording of a song with payment to be made to the recording studio, musicians, and vocalists when a deal is consummated.

Split publishing. When the publishing rights to a song are divided among two or more publishers.

Staff writer. One who writes exclusively for a publishing firm and earns a salary in this capacity.

Standard. A song that continues to be popular for several years.

Statutory copyright. Status acquired by a composition when it is registered with the Copyright Office or is published with the proper copyright notice.

Studio. Place where a song is recorded.

Subpublisher. The company that publishes a song or catalog in a territory other than that under the domain of the original publisher.

Subpublishing. When the original publisher contracts his song or catalog to be handled by a foreign publisher for that territory.

Sweeten. The addition of new parts to existing rhythm and vocal tracks such as strings and horns.

Synchronization. The placing of music in timed-relation to film.

Synchronization right. The right to use a musical composition in (timed-relation to) a film or video-tape.

Take. An attempt at putting down a track; an accepted recording of a musical or vocal section.

Top 40. Radio station format where records played are only those contained in lists of the best-selling records.

Top 100. Lists published in the trades of the top-selling singles for a particular market.

Track. One of the several components of special recording tape that contains recorded sounds, which is mixed with the other tracks for a finished recording of the song; the recording of all the instruments or vocals of a particular musical section; music and/or voices previously recorded.

Trades. Music industry publications.

Union scale. Minimum wage scale earned in employment by members of AFTRA, AF of M, SAG, etc.

Verse. The section of a song that precedes the chorus or is the A section in AABA pattern songs.

Appendix B: Exercises in Writing Lyrics, Melody, and Jingles

HERE ARE a few exercises devised to improve your skills in writing lyrics, music, and jingles. They should also serve as examples for you to create your own in any area you wish to develop your skill.

Exercises in Writing Lyrics

Exercise #1

The talented lyricist is versatile. He approaches lyric writing as a craft as well as a creative endeavor. He can write a clever lyric even about the most inanimate of subjects.

To improve your versatility and abilities, you should write every day. The theme or subject you use need not be ingenious, but your treatment of it should. The idea is for you to transform the dull, everyday object into the subject of an exciting story that will keep the listener's attention. A very successful song was ''Joy to the World,'' which had a bullfrog as one of its subjects.

Write a lyric about the following subjects (be sure to use a catchy title):

1. a bottle of wine
2. an old dog
3. an angel
4. a magician
5. a flower
6. a balloon

7. a candle   9. dynamite
8. a dancer   10. a city

Be flexible and vary your patterns. Write in AABA, ABAB, ABAC forms, etc. If you can become more creative in your writing about the inanimate, wait and see what you do to the subject of love!

Exercise #2

Write a lyric using the following titles:

1. "Get with It"
2. "Love Wakes Up with Me Each Morning"
3. "The Day Before I Die"
4. "Read All About It"
5. "How Can I Miss You If You Never Go Away"

Exercise #3

Use any of the following literary devices as the basis for the title and theme of a lyric:

1. Metaphor—the likening of one object to another ("He was a lion in combat.").
2. Euphemism—substitution of a mild or roundabout word or expression in place of one too distasteful ("Go fly a kite.").
3. Simile—a figure of speech expressing comparison by use of such terms as "like," "so," "or," "as" ("She is as sweet as candy.").
4. Satire—sarcasm, irony, or wit used to discredit folly and vice. ("She's a real nice girl"—appearing to mean "nice" but really meaning "easy.").
5. Onomatopoeia—words that sound like their natural sound (crack, bow-wow, zipper).

Exercise #4

Can you write verses to a given chorus? Try it! Write three verses to support the following chorus. It by no means constitutes a "hit" chorus, but merely serves as an exercise to get your creative juices flowing:

Title: "Everybody Wants to Smile"

Chorus: Everybody wants to smile
             but they all can't find the way

Everybody wants to smile
no they all can't find the way

Exercise in Writing Melody

Many songwriters write melodies by improvising around certain chord progressions. Improvisation is intrinsic to the jazz musician, which is perhaps why so many successful composers have their roots in jazz.

On page 143 are common chord progressions. Try to write a melody that fits their harmonic changes. Strive for naturalness and continuity in your melodies.

(Note: In the chord progressions, each slash mark equals one beat; a set of four slashes equals one bar.)

Exercise in Writing Jingles

Write a jingle for each of the following phrases by filling in a fictitious brand name in the blank space for the product specified and by composing a catchy melody to set to the phrase.

Light up your life with _____ (*cigarette*).

Spray once a day with _____ (*deodorant spray*).

Go to the head of the class with _____ (*shampoo*).

Go all the way in a _____ (*car*).

_____ makes waking up a pleasure (*coffee*).

Chord Progression #1

G	Em	Am	D D7	G G7	C Cm
/ / / /	/ / / /	/ / / /	/ / / /	/ / / /	/ / / /
A7	D7	Eb Cm	Bb7	Eb Cm	Bb7
/ / / /	/ / / /	/ / / /	/ / / /	/ / / /	/ / / /
Eb Cm	Bb7	Eb	D7	G	Em
/ / / /	/ / / /	/ / / /	/ / / /	/ / / /	/ / / /
Am	D D7	G G7	C Cm	A7 D7	G
/ / / /	/ / / /	/ / / /	/ / / /	/ / / /	/ / / /

Chord Progression #2

F	A7	Bb	Bbm	F	G7
/ / / /	/ / / /	/ / / /	/ / / /	/ / / /	/ / / /
Gm7	C7	F	F7	Bb	Bbm
/ / / /	/ / / /	/ / / /	/ / / /	/ / / /	/ / / /
F	G7	Gm7	C7	F	A7
/ / / /	/ / / /	/ / / /	/ / / /	/ / / /	/ / / /
Bb	Bbm	F	G7	Gm7 C7	F
/ / / /	/ / / /	/ / / /	/ / / /	/ / / /	/ / / /

Chord Progression #3

Bb	G7	C9	F7 Cm7 F7	Bb	G7
/ / / /	/ / / /	/ / / /	/ / / /	/ / / /	/ / / /
C9	F7	Dm	Eb	F7 Cm7	F7 Cm7
/ / / /	/ / / /	/ / / /	/ / / /	/ / / /	/ / / /
Eb	F7	Dm	F7	Bb	G7
/ / / /	/ / / /	/ / / /	/ / / /	/ / / /	/ / / /
C9	F7 Cm7 F7	Bb	G7	C9 F7	Bb
/ / / /	/ / / /	/ / / /	/ / / /	/ / / /	/ / / /

Appendix C:
Test Yourself

How MUCH of what you read did you learn? Remember, the educated songwriter will fare much better than the unlearned one. Take the following quiz and test your knowledge. The answers can be found in the respective question's chapter and if you miss any, go back and reread that chapter.

Here is how to score yourself:

0–6 correct answers—you bombed; go back to chapter 1.

7–15 correct answers—your song just got copyrighted.

16–22 correct answers—you got an appointment with a famous record producer.

23–28 correct answers—your song just got recorded.

29–30 correct answers—you earned a ''gold record.''

1. What are the four separate sources of income a musical copyright has?
2. What is a demo?
3. Explain an AABA pattern.
4. What is the function of an A & R director?
5. What are mechanical royalties?
6. What is a compulsory license?
7. What is the statutory term of copyright for a copyrighted song before and after January 1, 1978?
8. What is the role of the record producer?
9. What is a synchronization license?
10. What is a ''crossover''?
11. What is harmony?
12. Name three music trade publications.

13. What is a lead sheet?
14. Name four kinds of professional people you should submit your songs to.
15. Name two ways a song shark may operate.
16. What three elements are contained in the copyright notice?
17. What is a "hook"?
18. What is a master record?
19. What are the major three performing rights organizations in the United States?
20. What is the function of the music publisher?
21. Explain "pirating" and "bootlegging."
22. What two elements are examined in copyright infringement cases?
23. Why should you affiliate with a performing rights organization?
24. What are the three major categories of music that comprise the commercial music market?
25. (True or False) The money songwriters collect from the sale of a recording of their song is referred to as a performance royalty.
26. What is the statutory royalty rate for a recording of music sold before January 1, 1978, and after?
27. What is a "cover" record?
28. What is modulation?
29. Name four provisions the songwriter should attempt to have included in his songwriting contract.
30. What two basic rights must a motion picture producer acquire to music and lyrics in his film?

Appendix D:
Madison Avenue
and Beyond

THE FOLLOWING PAGES contain lists of several nationally known products with the advertising company's name and address that handles its accounts.

If you wish to write a jingle for one of the products, contact the advertising agency first, to be sure it still handles that account.

Accounts change very often but at the time this book went to press, this was the most up-to-date listing.

If you find a particular account has changed, check the *Standard Directory of Advertising Agencies* (National Register Publishing Co.), called the "Agency Red Book" in the trade, for the most recent listing. It is published yearly and is available at many local libraries, newspapers, and radio stations.

ADVERTISING AGENCIES

1. Carl Ally, 437 Madison Ave., New York, N.Y. 10022
2. N.W. Ayer, 1345 Ave. of the Americas, New York, N.Y. 10019
3. Ted Bates & Co., 1515 Broadway, New York, N.Y. 10036
4. BBDO, 383 Madison Ave., New York, N.Y. 10017
5. Benton & Bowles, 909 Third Ave., New York, N.Y. 10022
6. Bozell & Jacobs, 505 Park Ave., New York, N.Y. 10022
7. Leo Burnett U.S.A., Prudential Plaza, Chicago, Ill. 60601
8. Campbell-Ewald, 3044 West Grand Blvd., Detroit, Mich. 48202
9. Campbell-Mithun, Northstar Center, Minneapolis, Minn. 55402
10. Clyne Dusenberry, Inc., 245 Park Ave., New York, N.Y. 10017
11. Compton Advertising, 625 Madison Ave., New York, N.Y. 10022
12. Cunningham & Walsh, 260 Madison Ave., New York, N.Y. 10016
13. Dancer-Fitzgerald-Sample, 347 Madison Ave., New York, N.Y. 10017
14. Daniel & Charles, 261 Madison Ave., New York, N.Y. 10016
15. D'Arcy-MacManus & Masius, One Memorial Dr., St. Louis, Mo. 63102

16. W.B. Doner & Co., 26711 Northwestern Highway, Southfield, Mich. 48075
17. Doyle Dane Bernbach, 437 Madison Ave., New York, N.Y. 10017
18. DKG, Inc., 1271 Ave. of the Americas, New York, N.Y. 10019
19. Erwin Wasey, 5455 Wilshire Blvd., Los Angeles, Calif. 90036
20. William Esty, 100 East 42nd St., New York, N.Y. 10017
21. Foote, Cone & Belding, 200 Park Ave., New York, N.Y. 10017
22. Clinton E. Frank, 120 So. Riverside Plaza, Chicago, Ill. 60606
23. Gardner Advertising, 10 Broadway, St. Louis, Mo. 63102
24. Grey Advertising, Inc., 777 Third Ave., New York, N.Y. 10017
25. Kenyon & Eckhardt, 200 Park Ave., New York, N.Y. 10017
26. Ketchum, MacLeod & Grove, 4 Gateway Center, Pittsburgh, Pa. 15222
27. Lois Holland Calloway, 745 Fifth Ave., New York, N.Y. 10022
28. Marschalk, 1345 Avenue of the Americas, New York, N.Y. 10022
29. McCaffrey & McCall, 575 Lexington Ave., New York, N.Y. 10022
30. McCann-Erickson, 485 Lexington Ave., New York, N.Y. 10017
31. Arthur Meyerhoff, 410 N. Michigan Ave., Chicago, Ill. 60611
32. John F. Murray Advertising, 685 Third Ave., New York, N.Y. 10017
33. Needham, Harper & Steers, 909 Third Ave., New York, N.Y. 10022
34. Norman, Craig & Kummel, 919 Third Ave., New York, N.Y. 10022
35. Ogilvy & Mather, 2 East 48th St., New York, N.Y. 10017
36. Parkson Advertising, 767 Fifth Ave., New York, N.Y. 10022
37. SSC&B, One Dag Hammarskjold Plaza, New York, N.Y. 10017
38. Tatham-Laird & Kudner, 625 North Michigan Ave., Chicago, Ill. 60611
39. J. Walter Thompson Co., 420 Lexington Ave., New York, N.Y. 10017
40. Tracy-Locke, Box 50129, Dallas, Texas 75250
41. Warren, Muller, Dolobowsky, 747 Third Ave., New York, N.Y. 10017
42. Warwick, Welsh & Miller, 375 Park Ave., New York, N.Y. 10022
43. Wells, Rich, Greene, 767 Fifth Ave., New York, N.Y. 10022
44. Young & Rubicam, 285 Madison Ave., New York, N.Y. 10017

(The number listed with the following named products refers to the number of the advertising agency handling the product's advertising.)

PRODUCTS

A & P (30)
A T & T (2)
Absorbine Jr. (39)
Ac'cent (25)
AC-Delco (8)
Aetna Life (15)
Air France (25)
Air Jamaica (26)
Ajax (23)
Alitalia (19)
Alka Seltzer (43)
Alka - 2 (39)
All (37)
Amana (24)
American Airlines (17)
American Dairy (15)
American Motors (11/12)
American Oil (15)
Amoco (15)
American Express (35)

Anacin (32)
Anheuser-Busch (15)
Arco (33)
Aqua Velva (36)
Elizabeth Arden (21)
Arm & Hammer (27)
Armour (21)
Arrid (3)
Aunt Jemima (39)
Avis (17)
Avon (35)
Ballentine Beer (13)
Ban & Ultra Ban (14)
Beechnut (13)
Best Foods (13) (30)
Bic Panty Hose (43)
Bic Pens (43)
Birdseye (44)
Bisodol (10)
Black Flag (10)
Block Drugs (24) (37)
Bold (24)
Borden Foods (8) (39)
Borden, Inc. (6)
Bounty (13)
Brach Candies (31)
Breck (4)
Bristol-Myers (3) (21)
 (23) (44)

Brylcreem (25)
Budweiser (15)
Bufferin (3)
Buick (30)
Burger Chef (15)
Burger King (39)
Burlington Indus. (17)
Cadillac (15)
Calgon (12)
Campbell Soups (4) (33)
Canada Dry (24)
Carnation (19)
Celanese (17)
Charmin (5)
Chevrolet (8)
Chevron (4)
Chase & Sanborn (3)
Chiclets (20)
Chiquita (44)
Chun King (38)
Chrysler (4)
Clairol (17)
Clorox (26)
Cloud 9 (21)
Coca Cola (30 (38)
Coffee Mate (19)
Cold Power (34)
Colgate-Palm. (3)(20)(34)
Colt 45 (16)

Coppertone (42)
Consolidated Cigar (18)
Corning Glass (18)
Country Time (35)
Cremora (33)
Crest (5)
Cricket (39)
Crisco (11)
Datril (3)
Del Monte (30)
Dentyne (3)
Dial Soap (21)
Diet Rite Cola (7)
Dow Chemical (16 (34)
Dristan (20)
Dr. Pepper (44)
Dr. Scholl (2)
Dupont (2)
Duracell (13)
Dynamo (15)
Eastern Airlines (44)
Easy Off (32)
Efferdent (3)
Egg Beaters (3)
Era Detergent (7)
Ever Ready (20)
Excedrin (44)
Ex-Cello (8)
Exxon (29)
Fab (20)
Fiat (1)
Fleischman's (39)
Florida Citrus (13)
Folgers Coffee (12)
Ford Corp. (25)
Ford Small Cars (39)
Franco-American (33)
Freedent Gum (31)
Frigidaire (33)
Frito-Lay (21)
GAF Corp. (14)
Gallo Wine (19)
GE (4) (24) (44)
General Cigar (44)
General Foods (5) (24)
  (35) (44)
General Mills (13)
  (33)
General Telephone (17)
General Tire (15)
Gerber Foods (15)
Geritol (36)
Gillette (24 (39)
Glad Wrap (7)
Glamorene (35)
Gleem (7)
Gold Medal (13)
Good Seasons (35)

Goodyear (2) (8)
Gravy Train (5)
Great Beginnings (39)
Green Giant (7)
Greyhound (24)
Gulf Oil (19) (44)
Haley's M-O (27)
Hallmark Cards (21)
Halo - (20)
Handler Shampoo (39)
Hanes L'Eggs (13)
Hardees Foods (5)
Hawaiian Punch (4)
Heinz Foods (7) (26)
Hershey (35)
Hertz (3)
Heublein's (28)
H-O Cereals (37)
Holland House (21)
Honda (33)
Hormel Foods (4)
Hunt-Wesson (26)
IBM (1) (11)
Interwoven (14)
Irish Spring (20)
Jack-in-the-Box (17)
Jaguar Cars (6)
Jeep (11)
Jello (44)
Jergens (12)
Johnson & Johnson (11)
  (44)
Johns-Manville (44)
Joy (24)
Kal Kan (3)
Keds (30)
Kelloggs (4) (7)
Ken-L Ration (39)
Kimberly-Clark (7)
Kimbies (21)
Kleenex (7)
Kodak (39)
Koogle Pudding (33)
Kool Aid (24)
Kraft (21) (33) (39)
Kroger (9)
Lady Remington (18)
Lancers (30)
Lavoris (34)
Lehn & Fink (42)
Lestoil (21)
Lever Bros. (35) (37)
Lifebuoy (37)
Life Savers (13)
Lincoln-Mercury (25)
Lipton (37) (44)
Listerine (39)
Longines (35)

L'Oreal (30)
Love Cosmetics (43)
Lustre Creme (15)
Lux (39)
Lysol (37)
M & M (3)
Magnavox (20)
Man Power (25)
Marriott's (22)
Mattel (35)
Maxim (35)
Maxwell House (35)
Oscar Mayer (22)
Maytag (7)
Mazda Cars (21)
McDonalds (33)
Mennen (24) (41)
Michelob (15)
Midas (43)
Miles Lab. (38) (43)
Miller Beer (30)
Minute Maid (28)
Miracle Whip (33)
Mitchum (28)
Mobil Gasoline (17)
Morton Foods (24)
Mortons Salt (33)
Mountain Bell Tel. (40)
Mrs. Weaver's (22)
My-T-Fine (38)
Nabisco (3) (20) (35)
Neo-Synephrine (41)
Nescafe (7)
Nestle Products (2)
No Nonsense Hose (24)
Norelco (29)
Northeastern Mutual (39)
Northwest Orient (9)
Noxell (27)
Noxema (37)
Nytol (4)
Ocean Spray (3)
Old Milwaukee (12)
Oldsmobile (7)
Old Spice (34)
One-A-Day (39)
Ovaltine (18)
Pabst Beer (25)
Palmolive (15)
Pan-American Air (1)
Panasonic (3)
Paper-Mate (4)
Parker Pens (39)
Pazzazz (36)
J.C. Penney (29)
Pepperidge Farms (35)
Pepsi-Cola (4)
Pepto Bismol (5)

Appendix E:

Directory of Music Associations, Professional Organizations, and Licensing Organizations

American Composers Alliance (ACA)
   170 West 74th Street
   New York, N.Y. 10023

American Federation of Musicians (AF of M)
   1500 Broadway
   New York, N.Y. 10036

American Federation of Television and Radio Artists (AFTRA)
   1350 Avenue of the Americas
   New York, N.Y. 10019

American Guild of Authors and Composers (AGAC)
   40 West 57th Street
   New York, N.Y. 10019

   6430 Sunset Boulevard
   Hollywood, Calif. 90028

American Guild of Music
   P.O. Box 3
   Downers Grove, Ill. 60515

American Guild of Variety Artists (AGVA)
   1540 Broadway
   New York, N.Y. 10036

American Mechanical Rights Association (AMRA)
   250 West 57th Street
   New York, N.Y. 10019

American Music Center, Inc.
   250 West 57th Street
   Suite 626–7
   New York, N.Y. 10019

American Society of Composers, Authors and Publishers (ASCAP)
   1 Lincoln Plaza
   New York, N.Y. 10023 (headquarters)

   6430 Sunset Boulevard
   Suite 1002
   Hollywood, Calif. 90028

   2 Music Square West
   Nashville, Tenn. 37203

Equitable Life Building *
Room 1020
Montgomery Street
San Francisco, Calif. 94104

1065 NE 125th Street *
North Miami, Fla. 33161

1 Perimeter Way NW,*
Suite 415
Atlanta, Ga. 30339

645 North Michigan Avenue *
Suite 1000
Chicago, Ill. 60611

International Trade Mart Building *
Suite 1322
New Orleans, La. 70130

Park Square Building *
31 St. James Avenue
Boston, Mass. 02116

208–20 Greenfield *
Suite 305/North Section
Oak Park, Mich. 48237

7850 Metro Parkway *
Suite 106
Minneapolis, Minn. 55402

772 Hanna Building *
Playhouse Square
Cleveland, Ohio 44115

Benjamin Fox Pavillion *
Old York Road
Jenkintown, Pa. 19046

Communications Center *
Suite 340
3901 Westheimer
Houston, Tex. 77027

Broadcast Music, Inc. (BMI)
40 West 57th Street
New York, N.Y. 10019 (headquarters)

* Licensing office only.

6255 Sunset Boulevard
Hollywood, Caiif. 90028

10 Music Square East
Nashville, Tenn. 37203

888 Worcester Road *
Wellesley, Mass. 02181

1320 South Dixie Highway *
Coral Gables, Fla. 33146

230 North Michigan Avenue *
Chicago, Ill. 60601

3115 West Loop South *
Houston, Tex. 77027

BMI Canada, Limited (separate entity
from Broadcast Music, Inc.)
41 Valleybrook Drive
Don Mills
Ontario

1462 West Pender Street
Vancouver 5, B.C.

Canadian Musical Reproduction Rights
Agency, Ltd. (CMRRA)
198 Davenport Road
Toronto, Ontario M5R IJ2

Composers, Authors and Publishers
Association of Canada, Ltd. (CAPAC)
1240 Bay Street
Toronto, Ontario M5R 2C2

Composers and Lyricists Guild of
America (CLGA)
6565 Sunset Boulevard
Suite 420
Hollywood, Calif. 90028

Copyright Service Bureau Limited
(CSB)
221 West 57th Street
New York, N.Y. 10019

Country Music Association, Inc.
7 Music Circle North
Nashville, Tenn. 37203

Country Music Foundation, Inc.
4 Music Square East
Nashville, Tenn. 37203

Dramatists Guild, Inc.
234 West 44th Street
New York, N.Y., 10036

Gospel Music Association
38 Music Square West
Nashville, Tenn. 37203

Harry Fox Agency, Inc.
110 East 59th Street
New York, N.Y. 10022

Jazz Composers' Orchestra Association, Inc. (JCOA)
6 West 95th Street
New York, N.Y. 10025

The Martha Baird Rockefeller Fund for Music, Inc.
1 Rockefeller Plaza
Room 3315
New York, N.Y. 10020

Mietus Copyright Management
527 Madison Avenue
New York, N.Y. 10022

Music Publishers' Association of the U.S., Inc.
810 Seventh Avenue
New York, N.Y. 10019

Nashville Songwriters Association, International
25 Music Square West
Nashville, Tenn. 37203

National Academy of Recording Arts and Sciences (NARAS)
4444 Riverside Drive
Suite 202
Burbank, Calif. 91505

14 East 53rd Street
New York, N.Y. 10022

Suite 6505
505 N. Lake Shore Drive
Chicago, Ill. 60611

1227 Spring Street N.W.
Atlanta, Ga. 30309

639 Madison Avenue
Memphis, Tenn. 38103

7 Music Circle North
Nashville, Tenn. 37203

229 Shipley Street
San Francisco, Calif. 94107

National Association for American Composers USA (NAACUSA)
P.O. Box 49652
Barrington Station
Los Angeles, Calif. 90049

National Endowment for the Arts
806 15th Street NW
Washington, D.C. 20506

National Federation of Music Clubs
310 South Michigan Avenue
Suite 1936
Chicago, Ill. 60604

National Music Publishers Association
110 East 59th Street
New York, N.Y. 10022

One World of Music
1155 N. LaCienega Boulevard
Room 805
Los Angeles, Calif. 90069

Overseas Music Services, Inc.
   30 Rockefeller Plaza
   Suite 4535
   New York, N.Y. 10020

Paradisco Inc.
   71 East Avenue
   Norwalk, Conn. 06851

Radio Registry
   850 Seventh Avenue
   New York, N.Y. 10019

Recording Industry Association
of America (RIAA)
   1 East 57th Street
   New York, N.Y. 10022

   9200 Sunset Blvd.
   Suite 1005
   Los Angeles, Calif. 90069

SESAC Inc.
   10 Columbus Circle
   New York, N.Y. 10019

   11 Music Circle South
   Nashville, Tenn. 37203

Song Registration Service (SRS)
   6381 Hollywood Blvd.
   Suite 503
   Hollywood, Calif. 90028

Appendix F:
Directory of Music Publishers and Record Companies

THE FOLLOWING IS a list of the nation's top music publishers and record companies compiled from the most successful ones listed on the charts. You should submit your material to these firms in the professional manner as previously explained. For your convenience, the companies have been categorized by the type of music with which they have had the most success.

Music Publishers: Pop/Rhythm & Blues

Fred Ahlert Music Corp.
9165 Sunset Blvd.
Los Angeles, Calif. 90069

Almo/Irving (*see Rondor*)

Alouette Productions, Inc.
1650 Broadway
New York, N.Y. 10019

American Broadcasting Music, Inc.
11538 San Vincente Blvd.
Los Angeles, Calif. 90049

April/Blackwood Music, Inc.
51 West 52nd St.
New York, N.Y. 10019

6430 Sunset Blvd.
Hollywood Calif. 90028

Arc Music Corp.
110 East 59th St.
New York, N.Y. 10022

ATV Music Corp.
6255 Sunset Blvd.
Hollywood, Calif. 90028

1370 Avenue of the Americas
New York, N.Y. 10019

Barton Music Corp.
249 E. 62nd St.
New York, N.Y. 10021

9220 Sunset Blvd.
Los Angeles, Calif. 90069

Beechwood Music Corp.
1750 N. Vine St.
Hollywood, Calif. 90028

Belwin-Mills Publishing Corp.
16 West 61st St.
New York, N.Y. 10023

Bicycle Music Co.
8756 Holloway Dr.
Los Angeles, Calif. 90067

Big Pumpkin Music
75 Rockefeller Plaza
New York, N.Y. 10023

Big Seven Music Corp.
17 W. 60th St.
New York, N.Y. 10023

Boca Music, Inc.
532 Sylvan Ave.
Englewood Cliffs, N.J. 07632

Bourne Co.
1212 Avenue of the Americas
New York, N.Y. 10036

Braintree Music
1900 Avenue of the Stars
Los Angeles, Calif. 90067

Brut Music Publishing
1345 Avenue of the Americas
New York, N.Y. 10019

Buddah Music, Inc.
810 Seventh Ave.
New York, N.Y. 10019

Burlington Music Corp.
539 W. 25th St.
New York, N.Y. 10001

Bushka Music
1800 Century Park E.
Los Angeles, Calif. 90067

CAM-USA, Inc.
489 Fifth Ave.
New York, N.Y. 10017

Career/Arista Music Co.
9220 Sunset Blvd.
Los Angeles, Calif. 90069

Caseyem Music
9255 Sunset Blvd.
Los Angeles, Calif. 90069

Chappell Music Co.
810 Seventh Ave.
New York, N.Y. 10019

6255 Sunset Blvd.
Hollywood, Calif. 90028

Charing Cross Music, Inc.
36 E. 61st St.
New York, N.Y. 10021

Cherry Lane Music Co.
P.O. Box 4247
Greenwich, Conn. 06830

Chrysalis Music Corp.
360 E. 65th St.
New York, N.Y. 10021

Claridge Music
6381 Hollywood Blvd.
Hollywood, Calif. 90028

Combine Music Corp.
35 Music Square East
Nashville, Tenn. 37203

Don Costa Productions
9229 Sunset Blvd.
Los Angeles, Calif. 90069

Cotillion Music, Inc.
75 Rockefeller Plaza
New York, N.Y. 10019

Crazy Cajun
5626 Brock
Houston, Tex. 77023

Criterion Music Corp.
6124 Selma Ave.
Hollywood, Calif. 90028

17 W. 60th St.
New York, N.Y. 10023

Curtom/Gemingo
5915 N. Lincoln Ave.
Chicago, Ill. 60659

Darla Music, Inc.
4507 Carpenter Ave.
N. Hollywood, Calif. 91607

Dawnbreaker Music Co.
6430 Sunset Blvd.
Hollywood, Calif. 90028

Delightful Music Co., Ltd.
200 W. 57th St.
New York, N.Y. 10019

Dozier Music, Inc.
8467 Beverly Blvd.
Los Angeles, Calif. 90048

Dunbar Music, Inc.
1133 Avenue of the Americas
New York, N.Y. 10036

6363 Sunset Blvd.
Hollywood, Calif. 90028

The Entertainment Co.
40 W. 57th St.
New York, N.Y. 10019

Equinox Music
9220 Sunset Blvd.
Los Angeles, Calif. 90069

Fame Publishing Co., Inc.
603 E. Avalon Ave.
Muscle Shoals, Ala. 35660

Famous Music Corp.
1 Gulf & Western Plaza
New York, N.Y. 10023

6430 Sunset Blvd.
Hollywood, Calif. 90028

Far Out Music, Inc.
7417 Sunset Blvd.
Hollywood, Calif. 90046

Wes Farrell Organization
9200 Sunset Blvd.
Hollywood, Calif. 90069

Filmways Music Publishing, Inc.
1800 Century Park E.
Los Angeles, Calif. 90067

Fort Knox Music Co.
1619 Broadway
New York, N.Y. 10019

Frank Music Corp.
119 W. 57th St.
New York, N.Y. 10019

Fullness Music Co.
6922 Hollywood Blvd.
Hollywood, Calif. 90028

Al Gallico Music Corp.
65 W. 55th St.
New York, N.Y. 10019

6255 Sunset Blvd.
Los Angeles, Calif. 90028

Garrett Music Enterprises
6255 Sunset Blvd.
Los Angeles, Calif. 90028

Gaucho Music
161 W. 54th St.
New York, N.Y. 10019

Gil Music Corp.
1650 Broadway
New York, N.Y. 10019

Green Menu Music Co.
50 W. 57th St.
New York, N.Y. 10019

T. B. Harms Co.
100 Wilshire Blvd.
Santa Monica, Calif. 90401

6255 Sunset Blvd.
Hollywood, Calif. 90028

200 W. 57th St.
New York, N.Y. 10019

Hill and Range Songs, Inc. (*see Chappell*)

Tash Howard Music Group
1697 Broadway
New York, N.Y. 10019

Hudson Bay Music Co.
1619 Broadway
New York, N.Y. 10019

Island Music
7720 Sunset Blvd.
Los Angeles, Calif. 90046

Dick James Music, Inc.
119 W. 57th St.
New York, N.Y. 10019

Jobete Music Co. Inc.
6255 Sunset Blvd.
Hollywood, Calif. 90028

157 W. 57th St.
New York, N.Y. 10019

Julio-Brian Music, Inc.
888 Seventh Ave.
New York, N.Y. 10019

Kamakazi Music Corp.
1650 Broadway
New York, N.Y. 10019

KasKat Music, Inc.
323 E. Shore Rd.
Great Neck, N.Y. 11023

Keca Music, Inc.
7033 Sunset Blvd.
Hollywood, Calif. 90028

Don Kirshner Music, Inc.
1370 Avenue of the Americas
New York, N.Y. 10019

Lowery Group
P.O. Box 9687
1224 Fernwood Circle
Atlanta, Ga. 30319

Malaco Music Co.
3023 W. Northside Dr.
Jackson, Miss. 39213

E. B. Marks Music Corp.
1790 Broadway
New York, N.Y. 10019

MCA Music
445 Park Ave.
New York, N.Y. 10022

1777 N. Vine St.
Hollywood, Calif. 90028

Midsong Music International, Ltd.
1650 Broadway
New York, N.Y. 10019

Mighty Three Music, Inc.
309 S. Broad St.
Philadelphia, Pa. 19107

Ivan Mogull Music Corp.
40 E. 49 St.
New York, N.Y. 10017

E. H. Morris & Co., Inc.
810 Seventh Ave.
New York, N.Y. 10019

Muscle Shoals Sound Publishing Co.,
Inc.
3614 Jackson Hwy.
Sheffield, Ala. 35660

Music Music Music Inc.
157 W. 57th St.
New York, N.Y. 10019

No Exit Music Co., Inc.
535 Cotton Ave.
Macon, Ga. 31201

Organic Management
745 Fifth Ave.
New York, N.Y. 10022

Peer-Southern Organization
1740 Broadway
New York, N.Y. 10019

6922 Hollywood Blvd.
Los Angeles, Calif. 90028

Pickwick International, Inc.
135 Crossways Park Dr.
Woodbury, N.Y. 11797

Playboy Music Publishing Co.
8560 Sunset Blvd.
Los Angeles, Calif. 90069

Rondor Music, Inc.
1416 N. La Brea Ave.
Hollywood, Calif. 90028

RSO
135 Central Park West
New York, N.Y. 10023

David Rubinson & Friends, Inc.
1550 Market St.
San Francisco, Calif. 94102

A. Schroeder International, Ltd.
25 W. 56th St.
New York, N.Y. 10019

Screen Gems-EMI Music, Inc.
711 Fifth Ave.
New York, N.Y. 10022

7033 Sunset Blvd.
Hollywood, Calif. 90028

Larry Shayne Music, Inc.
6290 Sunset Blvd.
Hollywood, Calif. 90028

15 E. 48th St.
New York, N.Y. 10017

Sherlyn Publishing Co.
495 SE 10 Court
Hialeah, Fla. 33010

Silver Blue Music
401 E. 74th St.
New York, N.Y. 10021

Creed Taylor, Inc.
1 Rockefeller Plaza
New York, N.Y. 10020

Tree Publishing Co., Inc.
P.O. Box 1273
8 Music Square West
Nashville, Tenn. 37202

TRO
10 Columbus Circle
New York, N.Y. 10019

Twentieth Century Music Corp.
8544 Sunset Blvd.
Los Angeles, Calif. 90069

United Artists Music Publishing Group, Inc.
6920 Sunset Blvd.
Los Angeles, Calif. 90028

729 Seventh Ave.
New York, N.Y. 10019

Warner Bros. Music
9200 Sunset Blvd.
Hollywood, Calif. 90069

75 Rockefeller Plaza
New York, N.Y. 10019

Music Publishers: Country and Western

Abingdon Press
201 Eighth Ave. South
Nashville, Tenn. 37202

Acoustic Music, Inc.
5304 Camelot Court
Brentwood, Tenn. 37027

Acuff-Rose Publications, Inc.
2510 Franklin Rd.
Nashville, Tenn. 37204

Ahab Music Co., Inc.
1707 Grand Ave.
Nashville, Tenn. 37212

American Broadcasting Music, Inc.
2409 21 Ave. South
Nashville, Tenn. 37212

American Cowboy Music Co.
11 Music Circle South
Nashville, Tenn. 37203

Americus Music
44 Music Square East
Nashville, Tenn. 37203

ATV Music Corp.
55 Music Square West
Nashville, Tenn. 37203

Baron Music Publishing Co.
916 19 Ave. South
Nashville, Tenn. 37212

Beechwood Music Corp.
1014 17 Ave. South
Nashville, Tenn. 37212

Blue Book Music
1225 N. Chester Ave.
Bakersfield, Calif. 93308

Blue Echo Music
1104 18 Ave. South
Nashville, Tenn. 37212

Buckhorn Music Publishers, Inc.
1007 17 Ave. South
Nashville, Tenn. 37212

Glen Campbell Music, Inc.
10920 Wilshire Blvd.
Los Angeles, Calif. 90024

Buzz Cason Publications
2804 Azalea Place
Nashville, Tenn. 37204

Cedarwood Publishing Co., Inc.
815 16th Ave. South
Nashville, Tenn. 37203

Chappell Music Co.
1512 Hawkins St.
Nashville, Tenn. 37203

Cherry Lane Music Co.
P.O. Box 4247
Greenwich, Conn. 06830

Coal Miners Music, Inc.
7 Music Circle North
Nashville, Tenn. 37203

Combine Music Corp.
35 Music Square East
Nashville, Tenn. 37203

Danor Music, Inc.
1800 Grand Ave.
Nashville, Tenn. 37212

Debdave Music, Inc.
P.O. Box 2154
Nashville, Tenn. 37214

Dunbar Music, Inc.
1605 Hawkins St.
Nashville, Tenn. 37203

Evil Eye Music Co.
10 Columbus Circle
New York, N.Y. 10019

Famous Music Corp.
2 Music Circle South
Nashville, Tenn. 37203

Four Star Music Co., Inc.
49 Music Square West
Nashville, Tenn. 37203

Al Gallico Music Corp.
1207 16th Ave. South
Nashville, Tenn. 37212

Golden Horn Music, Inc.
50 Music Square West
Nashville, Tenn. 37203

Hallnote Music
P.O. Box 40209
Nashville, Tenn. 37204

Jim Halsey Co., Inc.
901 18th Ave. South
Nashville, Tenn. 37212

T. B. Harms Co.
P.O. Box 1026
11 Music Circle South
Nashville, Tenn. 37202

House of Bryant Publications
P.O. Box 36
Hendersonville, Tenn. 37075

House of Cash, Inc.
P.O. Box 508
Hendersonville, Tenn. 37075

House of Gold Music, Inc.
P.O. Box 50338
Belle Meade Station
Nashville, Tenn. 37205

Jack & Bill Music Co.
11 Music Circle South
Nashville, Tenn. 37202

Jack Music, Inc.
P.O. Box 1333
Nashville, Tenn. 37202

Keca Music, Inc.
7033 Sunset Blvd.
Hollywood, Calif. 90028

Lowery Group
P.O. Box 9687
1224 Fernwood Circle
Atlanta, Ga. 30319

Mariposa Music, Inc.
713 18th Ave. South
Nashville, Tenn. 37203

Roger Miller's Music
1300 Division St.
Nashville, Tenn. 37203

Newkeys Music, Inc.
29 Music Square East
Nashville, Tenn. 37203

Owepar Publishing Co.
813 18th Ave. South
Nashville. Tenn. 37203

Peer-Southern Organization
7 Music Circle North
Nashville, Tenn. 37203

Ben Peters Music
900 Old Hickory Blvd.
Rt. 6
Brentwood, Tenn. 37027

Pi-Gem Music, Inc.
1225 16th Ave. South
Nashville, Tenn. 37204

Prima-Donna Music Co.
1225 16th Ave. South
Nashville, Tenn. 37212

Sawgrass Music Publishers, Inc.
1722 West End Ave.
Nashville, Tenn. 37203

Screen Gems-EMI Music, Inc.
1207 16th Ave. South
Nashville, Tenn. 37212

Shade Tree Music
P.O. Box 842
Bakersfield, Calif. 93302

Shelby Singleton Music, Inc.
3106 Belmont Blvd.
Nashville, Tenn. 37212

Tree Publishing Co., Inc.
P.O. Box 1273
8 Music Square West
Nashville, Tenn. 37202

Twitty Bird Publishing Co.
708 17th Ave. South
Nashville, Tenn. 37202

Hank Williams Jr. Music, Inc.
806 16th Ave. South
Nashville, Tenn. 37203

Window Music Publishing Co., Inc.
809 18th Ave. South
Nashville, Tenn. 37203

Word, Inc.
4800 West Waco Drive
Waco, Tex. 76710

Record Companies: Pop/Rhythm & Blues

ABC Records
8255 Beverly Blvd.
Los Angeles, Calif. 90048

1414 Avenue of the Americas
New York, N.Y. 10019

A & M Records, Inc.
    1416 North La Brea Ave.
    Los Angeles, Calif. 90028

    595 Madison Ave.
    New York, N.Y. 10022

Ariola America Inc.
    8671 Wilshire Blvd.
    Beverly Hills, Calif. 90211

Arista Records, Inc.
    6 West 57th St.
    New York, N.Y. 10019

    9220 Sunset Blvd.
    Los Angeles, Calif. 90069

Atlantic Recording Corp.
    75 Rockefeller Plaza
    New York, N.Y. 10019

    9229 Sunset Blvd.
    Los Angeles, Calif. 90069

ATV Records, Inc.
    3 West 57th St.
    New York, N.Y. 10019

Bang/Bullet Records, Inc.
    2107 Faulkner Rd. NE
    Atlanta, Ga. 30324

Barnaby Records, Inc.
    816 North La Cienega Blvd.
    Los Angeles, Calif. 90069

Bearsville Records, Inc.
    75 East 55th St.
    New York, N.Y. 10022

Big Tree Enterprises, Ltd.
    75 Rockefeller Plaza
    New York, N.Y. 10019

Brunswick Record Corp.
    888 Seventh Ave.
    New York, N.Y. 10019

    1449 South Michigan Ave.
    Chicago, Ill. 60605

Buddah/Kama Sutra Records, Inc.
    810 Seventh Ave.
    New York, N.Y. 10019

    9255 Sunset Blvd.
    Los Angeles, Calif. 90069

CBS Records
    51 West 52nd St.
    New York, N.Y. 10019

Capitol Records, Inc.
    1750 North Vine St.
    Hollywood, Calif. 90028

    1370 Avenue of the Americas
    New York, N.Y. 10019

Capricorn Records, Inc.
    535 Cotton Ave.
    Macon, Ga. 31208

    4405 Riverside Dr.
    Burbank, Calif. 91505

Caribou Records
    8500 Melrose Ave.
    Los Angeles, Calif. 90069

Casablanca Records, Inc.
    8255 Sunset Blvd.
    Los Angeles, Calif. 90046

Chrysalis Records, Inc.
    9255 Sunset Blvd.
    Los Angeles, Calif. 90069

Claridge Records
    6381 Hollywood Blvd.
    Hollywood, Calif. 90028

Columbia (*see CBS*)

De-Lite Records Sound Corp.
200 West 57th St.
New York, N.Y. 10019

Elektra/Asylum Records
962 North La Cienega Blvd.
Los Angeles, Calif. 90069

665 Fifth Ave.
New York, N.Y. 10019

Epic (*see CBS*)

Fantasy/Prestige/Milestone Records
10 and Parker Sts.
Berkeley, Calif. 94710

Wes Farrell Organization
9200 Sunset Blvd.
Los Angeles, Calif. 90069

GNP Crescendo Records
8560 Sunset Blvd.
Los Angeles, Calif. 90069

Granite Records
6255 Sunset Blvd.
Los Angeles, Calif. 90028

1370 Avenue of the Americas
New York, N.Y. 10019

Haven Records, Inc.
6255 Sunset Blvd.
Hollywood, Calif. 90028

Hi Recording Corp.
308 Poplar Ave.
Memphis, Tenn. 38103

H & L Records Corp.
532 Sylvan Ave.
Englewood Cliffs, N.J. 07632

Island Records, Inc.
7720 Sunset Blvd.
Los Angeles, Calif. 90046

154 West 57th St.
New York, N.Y. 10019

Janus Records (Div. of GRT Corp.)
8776 Sunset Blvd.
Los Angeles, Calif. 90069

Kirshner Entertainment Corp.
1370 Avenue of the Americas
New York, N.Y. 10019

Lifesong Records, Inc.
488 Madison Ave.
New York, N.Y. 10022

9229 Sunset Blvd.
Los Angeles, Calif. 90069

London Records, Inc.
539 West 25th St.
New York, N.Y. 10001

Magna Glide Record Corp.
323 East Shore Rd.
Great Neck, N.Y. 11023

Mainstream Records, Inc.
1700 Broadway
New York, N.Y. 10019

Malaco, Inc.
3023 West North Side Dr.
Jackson, Miss. 39213

MCA Records, Inc.
100 Universal City Plaza
Universal City, Calif. 91608

445 Park Ave.
New York, N.Y. 10022

Mercury (*see Phonogram*)

MGM (*see Polydor, Inc.*)

Midsong International Records, Inc.
1650 Broadway
New York, N.Y. 10019

Motown Record Corp.
6255 Sunset Blvd.
Hollywood, Calif. 90028

Philadelphia International Records
309 South Broad St.
Philadelphia, Pa. 19107

Phonogram Inc./Mercury Records
1 IBM Plaza
Chicago, Ill. 60611

6255 Sunset Blvd.
Hollywood, Calif. 90028

110 West 57th St.
New York, N.Y. 10019

Pickwick International U.S.A.
135 Crossways Park Dr.
Woodbury, N.Y. 11797

Platinum Record Co., Inc.
96 West St.
Englewood, N.J. 07631

Playboy Records, Inc.
8560 Sunset Blvd.
Los Angeles, Calif. 90069

Polydor, Inc.
810 Seventh Ave.
New York, N.Y. 10019

7165 Sunset Blvd.
Los Angeles, Calif. 90046

Private Stock Records, Ltd.
40 West 57th St.
New York, N.Y. 10019

Ranwood Records, Inc.
9034 Sunset Blvd.
Los Angeles, Calif. 90069

RCA Records
1133 Avenue of the Americas
New York, N.Y. 10036

6363 Sunset Blvd.
Hollywood, Calif. 90028

Reprise (*see Warner Bros.*)

The Rocket Record Co.
211 South Beverly Dr.
Beverly Hills, Calif. 90212

Roulette Records, Inc.
17 West 60th St.
New York, N.Y. 10023

RSO Records and Tapes, Inc.
9200 Sunset Blvd.
Los Angeles, Calif. 90069

135 Central Park West
New York, N.Y. 10023

Salsoul-Salsa Records
240 Madison Ave.
New York, N.Y. 10016

Scepter Records, Inc.
254 West 54th St.
New York, N.Y. 10019

Shelter Recording Co., Inc.
5112 Hollywood Blvd.
Hollywood, Calif. 90027

Sire Records, Inc.
165 West 74th St.
New York, N.Y. 10023

Springboard International Records, Inc.
947 US HWY. 1
Rahway, N.J. 07065

Spring Records, Inc.
   161 West 54th St.
   New York, N.Y. 10019

Stanyan Record Co.
   8440 Santa Monica Blvd.
   Hollywood, Calif. 90069

Creed Taylor, Inc.
   1 Rockefeller Plaza
   New York, N.Y. 10020

TK Productions, Inc.
   495 SE 10 Court
   Hialeah, Fla. 33010

Tom Cat Records
   450 North Roxbury Dr.
   Beverly Hills, Calif. 90210

Twentieth Century Records
   8544 Sunset Blvd.
   Los Angeles, Calif. 90069

United Artists Records of America
   6920 Sunset Blvd.
   Los Angeles, Calif. 90028

   729 Seventh Ave.
   New York, N.Y. 10019

Vanguard Recording Society, Inc.
   71 West 23rd St.
   New York, N.Y. 10010

Virgin Records, Inc.
   55 West 53rd St.
   New York, N.Y. 10019

Warner Bros. Records, Inc.
   3300 Warner Blvd.
   Burbank, Calif. 91510

   44 East 50th St.
   New York, N.Y. 10022

WEA International, Inc.
   75 Rockefeller Plaza
   New York, N.Y. 10019

Wooden Nickel Records, Inc.
   6521 Homewood Ave.
   Los Angeles, Calif. 90028

Record Companies:
Country and Western

ABC/Dot Records, Inc.
   2409 21st Ave. South
   Nashville, Tenn. 37212

Barnaby Records
   816 N. La Cienega Blvd.
   Los Angeles, Calif. 90069

Brite-Star
   728 16th Ave. South
   Nashville, Tenn. 37203

Buddah/Kama Sutra Records, Inc.
   1701 West End
   Nashville, Tenn. 37203

Capitol Records, Inc.
   806 16th Ave. South
   Nashville, Tenn. 37203

Capricorn Records, Inc.
   535 Cotton Ave.
   Macon, Ga. 31208

CBS Records
   804 16th Ave. South
   Nashville, Tenn. 37203

Columbia (*see CBS*)

Epic (*see CBS*)

Goldmont Music, Inc.
  24 Music Square East
  Nashville, Tenn. 37203

Granite Records
  55 Music Square West
  Nashville, Tenn. 37203

GRT Records
  1226 16th Ave. South
  Nashville, Tenn. 37212

Hickory Records, Inc.
  2510 Franklin Rd.
  Nashville, Tenn. 37204

Hi Recording Corp.
  308 Poplar Ave.
  Memphis, Tenn. 38103

MCA Records, Inc.
  27 Music Square East
  Nashville, Tenn. 37203

Mercury (*see Phonogram*)

MGM (*see Polydor*)

Monument Record Corp.
  21 Music Square East
  Nashville, Tenn. 37203

Music City Workshop, Inc.
  38 Music Square East
  Nashville, Tenn. 37203

Music Mill, Inc.
  1108 East Avalon Ave.
  Muscle Shoals, Ala. 35660

  21 Music Circle East
  Nashville, Tenn. 37203

Nashville West Productions
  124 Country Side Dr.
  Bakersfield, Calif. 93308

Phonogram, Inc./Mercury Records
  10 Music Circle South
  Nashville, Tenn. 37203

Plantation Records
  3106 Belmont Blvd.
  Nashville, Tenn. 37212

Playboy Records, Inc.
  1300 Division St.
  Nashville, Tenn. 37203

Polydor/MGM Records, Inc.
  21 Music Circle East
  Nashville, Tenn. 37203

RCA Records
  806 17th Ave. South
  Nashville, Tenn. 37203

Rice Records, Inc.
  29 Music Square East
  Nashville, Tenn. 37203

Shannon Records, Inc.
  P.O. Drawer 1
  Madison, Tenn. 37115

Skylite-Sing, Inc.
  1008 17th Ave. South
  Nashville, Tenn. 37212

United Artists Records of America
  50 Music Square West
  Nashville, Tenn. 37203

Warner Bros. Records, Inc.
  P.O. Box 12646
  Nashville, Tenn. 37212

Word, Inc.
  4800 West Waco Dr.
  Waco, Tex. 76703

Index

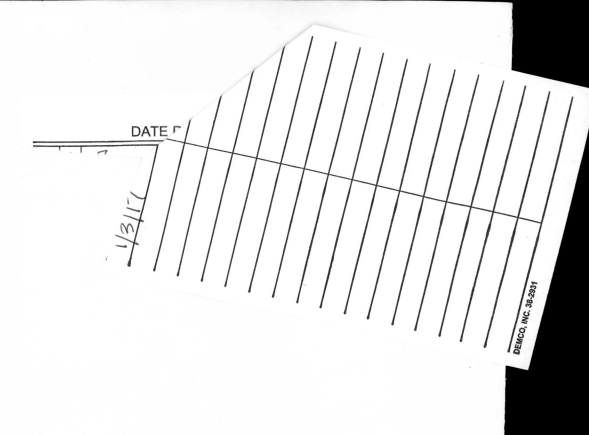

DATE

1/31/